# A Woman's Vault

## UNLOCKING THE 7 SECRETS
## TO A REMARKABLE LIFE

## ERIKA WALKER

# A Woman's Vault
## *Unlocking the 7 Secrets to a Remarkable Life*

by Erika Walker

ISBN 13: 978-1-944027-11-7 (paperback)
ISBN 13: 978-1-944027-10-0 (ebook)

Net(worlding
PUBLISHING

# CHAPTER ONE

# The History of Vaults

L ocks and keys existed long before mankind first used them, in both the spiritual world and in our physical and mental planes. In fact, both the Old and New Testaments refer to angels as "having the keys to heaven and hell" and "life and death." In fact, there are literally thousands of references throughout literature to the "keys" of knowledge. Apparently, even on the spiritual plane, securing things is important.

Further, locks to vaults and the keys that open them are *symbols* of opening and closing, of access and denial to access. Sometimes locks keep us out while other times, they keep us in. And at rare moments, a key can mean the difference between freedom and incarceration.

Keys also affect our daily lives. They give us security. We can lock our doors at night and know that no one else has the key. We can encrypt our emails, music, documents, videos, and all of our computer files with digital keys. We lock our phones, offices, cars, luggage, and bikes. More people have keys than cell phones. We are a society obsessed with protecting our valuables and ourselves. But that's not all.

It's been a century or two since men allegedly ensured their wives' chastity before they rode off to war knowing that their wives would not and *could not* have sex with another man because they'd been locked into a fabrication made of metal and leather called a "chastity belt." Fathers locked up their daughters' virginity, and kings their mistresses. And in a world where a son inherited the throne and royal bloodlines were considered divinely imbued, the chastity belt was used to ensure that a bastard child from an illicit affair could not hold the throne.

Historians have tried to debunk the story of the chastity belt for centuries, but stories about it persist. Although there is no historical evidence that they were ever widely used or even used at all, the stories themselves are a powerful commentary on the value of women's genitalia and their ability to bring life into the world. It's also a compelling illustration of the power of locks and keys to create and control empires. These belts demonstrated how both men and women believed that a woman's chastity, virginity, and potential to create life needed to be protected at all costs.

When most of us think of securing our valuables, our chastity probably isn't at the top of the list. Rather, we think of money, stocks, heirlooms, jewelry, silver, gold, photos, documents, etc.

In fact, the need for secure places to store those kinds of valuables stretches back for centuries. The Egyptians were the first to make locks, followed by the Romans, who created what were called *warded locks*. These locks were comprised of special notches and grooves similar to the locks of today that made picking them much more difficult. But what about the vaults or safes where the real treasures were stored?

Since the beginning of time, people have hidden treasures in plain sight, depending on human nature's tendency to overlook the obvious. The "Golden Buddha" story is one such example.

In 1957, a group of Thai monks learned their large clay Buddhist shrine was to be relocated to make way for a highway and other modern developments in the area. They would need to move the Buddha at their monastery to a new location.

On moving day, the clay Buddha was prepared for its journey. Calculations were made, and a large crane was brought in to lift the Buddha. As the crane struggled under the weight of the shrine, the Buddha began to crack. Apparently, the engineers had miscalculated the weight of the shrine. Or had they? The supervising monk frantically called to the crane operator to set the Buddha down so they could see how much damage had been done.

Several large cracks were found, causing the monk to shut down operations and request that the crew order a larger crane. The Buddha was left in an open courtyard. That wouldn't have been a problem on most days. However, a storm was brewing that night. So, the monks covered the Buddha with a waterproof tarp to keep it dry.

Even though the tarp was secure, the head monk woke up and decided to check on the shrine just to be sure. Flashlight in hand, the monk carefully walked around the huge clay figure, re-examining the cracks. As his flashlight moved over a larger crack, something shiny glinted back at him.

He peered into the crack and didn't understand the strange sight he was looking at. He returned to his room, found a chisel and hammer, and went back to the Buddha. He began carefully chipping at the clay around the crack. As the crack widened, he could not believe his eyes. He ran to wake the other monks. By lantern light, all the monks carefully chipped all the clay from the Buddha. Hours later, the monks stepped back and stared in awe at the sight before them.

There stood a solid gold Buddha.

When the moving crew arrived later that morning to complete the job of moving the Buddha to its new location, there was much confusion and excitement. Where had the clay Buddha gone? Where had the Golden Buddha come from? Historians were called, and research was begun to discover the origin of the Golden Buddha.

Slowly, the pieces of the story were put together. The Golden Buddha was the cherished responsibility of a group of monks charged with its protection several centuries earlier. When those monks received word that the Burmese army was headed their way, they were concerned that the invading army would loot the shrine for its Golden Buddha. Working quickly, the monks covered their Buddha with 8 to 12 inches of clay, making it simply appear to be made of clay.

The monks were sure that the army would have no interest in a clay Buddha, and they were right. However, the Burmese army did kill all of the monks before they moved on. Their secret died with them, and The Golden Buddha was lost in history until 1957.

So, whether mankind or angels created locks and keys, or whether we have found ways to "lock" treasure in plain sight, we still understand what it means to protect something of value in whatever way we can.

Anything we cherish, need, or possess can be hidden away and locked up for protection. Sometimes, we don't even recognize the sacred gifts we have, if like the golden Buddha, they're hidden in plain sight.

## YOUR VAULT

What I want to show you is that you have things of greater value inside of your metaphorical vault than you realize. The precious things in your vault are more valuable, powerful, and life altering than money, jewelry, or physical property. Unlike the thieves and robbers throughout history who could figure out how to break into the best of vaults, so many find it hard to reveal the treasures inside themselves.

This is especially true for women. So many of us are so focused on caring for others that we don't take the time to figure out our true selves. But I'm here to change that with this book. I'll share with you the seven secrets I've discovered that will help you realize your fullest potential, something every girl and woman deserves to achieve. We are a part of an important evolutionary shift. There is a need for recognizing our power as women to create the world we desire and the world that is needed for the good of the whole.

To this end, each chapter will detail one of the seven secrets to feminine power. I use the word *secrets* not because these things are unknown to the world, but because like the golden Buddha, they're hiding in plain sight. They're out there, but we don't see the value in them.

Because of constant demands from the outer world, you may have focused, drawn, and anchored the energy of your own life in external conditions that have become your problems and limitations. And, like many, you may have been unclear about your innate gifts and power, and been fooled by the history of male influence on the world. Now you can learn to leverage your feminine power to become all you can be.

There's no time like the present. Let's begin.

# CHAPTER TWO

# The Seven Secrets

A s a little girl, I had a vision that when I grew up I would help others, especially women. I can remember when I first was introduced through the television to Oprah. I remember thinking, "This is me. This is the kind of reach I want."

My purpose is about helping other women realize their full potential. I know that whatever I'm doing in this space, it's going to work out. I don't have any fear about it anymore. I am being guided by my Source and, as such, I won't fail.

Here are the seven secrets that I have received by a power greater than my own brain, and I believe it is very important for you as a woman to experience the things in life **you** choose while simultaneously helping to create a better world for all of us.

## SECRET #1: YOU HAVE SUPERPOWERS

Superheroes don't just exist in comic books, video games, and movies. We are all superheroes because we possess gifts that we can use to do extraordinary things. Women in particular carry with them similarities to the most famous and well-known female superhero of all time – Wonder Woman.

If you weren't aware of Wonder Woman's origins or her powers, here's your chance to learn that you have many of the same gifts she received at birth, including intuition, courage, and wisdom. Learn how female power is different from male power and how both are needed to create a whole, balanced human being. By the way, it's certainly no coincidence that during the time this book was written, *Wonder Woman*, the movie, created a new record opening weekend for a movie directed by a woman, bringing in $103.1 million.

### SECRET #2: NO SUPER HERO GOES IT ALONE

As much as we'd often like or prefer to *do it all ourselves*, it's not possible in today's world. Even with all the technology around us, we need other people. In fact, we need them now more than ever. There's just too much information to learn, carry, and apply ourselves. There are too many opportunities and possibilities to process alone. That's why networking matters. Don't groan. Even if you hate networking, these tips and stories will make you see it in a different light.

Networking isn't about swapping business cards at conferences, then throwing them in a drawer to be forgotten forever once you get home. Networking is about relationships—about helping, giving, caring, and being engaged in authentic ways with others. Learn what that looks like and how feminine power and our natural drive to connect and support motivate one of our greatest superpowers – relationship with our sisters.

### SECRET #3: DELIBERATELY CREATE YOUR REALITY

Creating your own reality is the stuff of sci-fi movies, woo-woo mystics, and psychics, right? Wrong. Being able to create your own reality *is* science. It may not be the science you learned in high school, but it is the advanced science of quantum physics, psychology, and string theory. Don't worry. Burning candles, chanting spells, or drinking foul tasting potions is not required.

The wisest, most influential people throughout time, including Buddha, Jesus Christ, Ralph Waldo Emerson, and Napoleon Hill, have shared this secret throughout time. Stanford psychologist Carol Dweck wrote a book about it, *The Happiness Advantage*. Dweck and her colleagues found that some people have a "fixed mindset" and believe that they cannot change their capabilities. Other people have a "growth mindset." The growers believe they can work toward improving themselves. The fixed mindset people cannot and do not. In this chapter, we will show you how to have a "growth mindset" to develop the reality you want to live, day in and day out.

### SECRET #4: IT'S NOT THE SPOON THAT BENDS, BUT YOU

You saw *The Matrix*, right? If not, it's time to rent it and watch it, several times if you need to. If you did, you understand that the reality we're in is easily altered through a classic feminine skill called perspective.

What are you really looking at? Is what you see before you the only reality or just one reality? There's an old story about six blind men. They're led to an elephant, asked to touch it (not knowing what it is) and to describe it. One grasps the elephant's trunk and says, "It's a huge snake!" Another touches the broad side of the elephant and says, "It's a huge wall of leather!" Another has the tail and describes it as a rope. Each man saw one part of what was in front of them. Their perspective, or ability to perceive truth, is colored by the information they don't have.

When we jump to conclusions or assume details we don't have, we create a misleading reality that obscures the truth. Miscalibrated perspective can cause confusion, as the above example demonstrates. In this chapter, we will show you how to harness perspective properly and use it to illuminate your reality.

### SECRET #5: SUCCESS COMES FROM LEADING WITH FEMININE POWER

For decades, when companies wanted to target women for their predominantly male product lines, they simply painted the product pink and created a feminine name for it. We then had pink guns, pink hammers, pink motorcycles, and even pink camouflage and golf clubs. But they were all built to suit men. It wasn't surprising that women soon stopped purchasing products by color. Instead, many started creating their own goods – designing, building and manufacturing tools, toys, gear, tech, clothing, and traditionally male products for female consumers and users. Their products weren't just pink knockoffs. They were specifically made for women.

The secret to leading people means more than slapping "feminine" or "female" on the method and expecting women to lead as men have. To be successful as a female leader using feminine power, you must understand that the skills, methods, approaches, and personality of a true female leader are not just versions of the male approach to leadership. Women have their own dynamic approach to leadership, and this chapter will teach you how to lead with your feminine power.

### SECRET #6: SHIFT INTO EXTREME SELF-CARE ASAP

When it comes to stress, many of us see only one of two routes available to alleviate it. The first is to tough it out. If we put our heads down and really *try*, through sheer grit and determination, we can surely achieve our goal. The second is to dedicate special time to pampering and physical relaxation, such as a spa day or massage once in a blue moon. Both approaches, however, miss the true power of self-care when applied daily and holistically.

In this chapter, we will show you why daily self-care matters, and why common approaches like "toughing it out" and "spa days" often miss the mark in alleviating stressful issues in life. Indeed, the prolonged stress caused by "toughing it out" can lead to heart attacks, strokes, major health issues, and a lower quality of life. Spa days, conversely, only treat the outside, and do so too sparingly. True self-care is ultimately holistic. It involves daily maintenance through exercise, diet, and meditation. By following the guidance set forth in this chapter, you can de-stress, relax, recharge, and revitalize your life.

### SECRET #7: IMAGINATION

Finally, we take you to the directional path that will help you transition from where you are now, to where you want to go or have wanted to go in your life. In this chapter, sharing this secret, I'll take your hand and walk along with you as your tour guide.

As Carl Sagan, the great scientist, stated, "Imagination will often carry us to worlds that never were. But without it we go nowhere." Einstein carried the power of imagination even further when he shared, "Your imagination is everything. It is the preview of life's coming attractions." Then we get a very powerful and practical view of imagination from

Stephen R. Covey of "The Seven Habits" super fame, "Live out of your imagination, not your history."

This secret will tap into the wisdom the above guiding quotes and others in this chapter to help you steer your way toward a rich-life journey, a journey that will not only surprise you, but also delight you.

Let's begin.

# CHAPTER THREE

# Secret #1: You Have Superpowers

Superheroes are generally known for one particular superpower, or for a small cluster of superpowers. Superman, for instance, can fly, and he possesses superhuman strength, speed, and eyesight. Spiderman can climb tall buildings and swing on a web. He also has a "spidey sense" that alerts him to danger.

What's important to know about superpowers is that it's not just men who have them. Women possess them, too. And, like their male counterparts, there are superpowers I believe all women share. There are also some powers that are unique to each woman. Each of us needs to discover what those powers are for ourselves.

This may seem impossible to conceive of or, perhaps, highly intimidating. But I urge you not to see this as a daunting quest. Rather, this chapter will lead you on an exciting adventure to uncovering your most dynamic superpowers and the ways you can harness them to create powerful change in your life.

## SUPERPOWERS

In the world of comic book superheroes, we see superpowers like flight, X-ray vision, speed, strength, laser vision, and more. But oddly enough, the most powerful of all superpowers isn't extreme abilities. It's feminine power. And even today, true feminine power is rare. Why?

In the 1930s, 40s, and 50s, most comic book superheroes were created by male writers and artists for a primarily male audience. They played more into the fantasy life of men and were less concerned about the reality of what a powerful woman really looked like or what she could do with her mind. Female superheroes were more about women's bodies, boobs, and butts than their creativity, wisdom, and feminine power, portrayed largely as love interests, femme fatales, or sources for male angst. But then, most men didn't understand there was such a thing as feminine power at that time. So they did what they could with what they had and created female characters from a male, masculine energy point of view.

Because most who created and wrote these characters were male, they devised women in their stories to look like a male fantasy of desire. This meant crafting women with huge, heaving breasts, classical beauty, and very sexualized bodies. During the advent of many popular comics in the 1940s, women in the real world were working jobs that were traditionally filled by men, something reflected by the female heroes in comics. But even then, Wonder Woman was only invited to the Justice League as a secretary. Sue Storm was the resident damsel-in-distress, and the Invisible Girl well into her 20s and 30s. And Jean Grey started her superhero career as the weakest of the X-Men, the majority of her powers lent to her by her male professor.

Even post-war and well into the 60s, women were growing up surrounded on all sides by the message that they had to be submissive, soft, and feminine. All these powerful superheroes they saw were drawn like pinups, acting more like a man's idea of what a woman was like rather than an actual woman. With the advent of second-wave feminism in the late 60s and 70s, the representation got better. Many big superhero titles—*X-Men* one of the most prominent among them—began introducing more female superheroes like Storm, Batgirl, and Ms. Marvel. However, their characterizations were still rocky. Although this new era of female superheroes was a far cry from the days when Wonder Woman lost her power when a man chained her hands together, their newfound strength was drawn from the same root that male heroes were: the ideas of masculine power.

Of course, even in this new era, female superheroes were still incredibly beautiful, endowed, and often drawn in positions that made it look like their backs were broken to show off their bodies. It was hard to reconcile the double standard, one that still exists today, but the progression of feminism inside and outside the comics industry sparked changes we're seeing more of today. In fact, Marvel Comic's new Director of Content and Character Development is a woman. Sana Amanat is making huge strides in developing powerful female superheroes. For example, she has co-created the first solo series to feature a Muslim female superhero, Ms. Marvel, which has "spark[ed] excitement and dialogue about identity and the Muslim American struggle."[1] Other notable changes include a run of the original X-Men title with a full female cast for the first time in history!

The number of women writing comics is increasing, and so is their power to shape the role of women in their medium. The question is: will they tap into women's feminine power, or will they merely replicate the past by making women act like men?

Let me step back and explain a very basic awareness that most of us, both men and women, intuitively understand and under which we operate: male energy is dominant, aggressive, protective, and strong. Male superheroes take that traditional male energy and amp it up a thousand percent.

Their male energy is an exaggerated version of the normal male energy. That's why they're "superheroes." Superman, for instance, has more muscles, more strength, more speed, more courage, more of everything many men fantasize about having. Superman is the role model for many men. If you look at the average male superhero, you'll notice he rarely dips into his feminine side. They do show it from time to time to advance a storyline, but it's not a large part of a male superhero's personality.

Female energy, the Yin to the male Yang, is opposite that of the dominant male energy. Feminine energy is that of surrender. Before you see that as a negative, (as many do—assuming surrender means weakness) step back. Male and female energy is like the positive and negative energy on a battery. For an electrical circuit to be complete, you have to have a

---

1   https://about.me/sana_amanat.

positive and negative terminal. Everything in life requires a positive and negative charge. That "spark" or chemistry we feel with a certain person? That's our energy circuit being completed. We are literally feeling an energetic connection with that person because our energies complement each other, completing the circuit.

As a society, over time we have learned to value male energy and to devalue female energy. There's a whole book to be written on that, but let's just briefly look at what male and female energy are, and why we need both energies in life.

Masculine energy can be defined by the following qualities:

- Strong
- Linear
- Directed
- Steady
- Focused on one thing at a time
- Purposeful
- Assertive
- Aggressive
- Dominant
- Controlling
- Simple
- Compact
- Dense
- Conquering
- Predictable
- Fearless
- Likes to simplify
- Deals in uncomplicated problems

Female energy, on the other hand, can be defined by the following qualities:

- Gentle
- Soft
- Creative

- Curved
- Flowing
- Complex
- Multi-layered
- Protective
- Energized
- Fast
- Fluid
- Surrenders
- Needs to feel safe
- Adaptive
- Expansive
- Radiates
- Multi-tasks
- Emotional
- Feels deeply
- Talkative

Women as women, and men as men, need to have both energies to be in balance and tapped into our full potential. Masculine energy without feminine energy is not whole; and female energy without masculine energy is not complete. One without the other results in our not feeling valued or realized. We need both energies in our internal *and* external lives to feel strong, powerful, nurtured, and appreciated.

As women, we don't have to act like men to be powerful. In fact, we're more powerful if we don't. Our creative intuitive powers, our ability to network, to create relationships, to connect, to make others (particularly men) feel safe and connected to their own power is what makes us superheroes – *if* we learn to recognize and tap into that aspect of ourselves. The strongest power we have as women is the ability to surrender. Now, the word 'surrender' feels very weak, but that's the Golden Buddha under the clay! When we surrender to someone else, we enhance our power because we become open to possibilities and give up the need to control everything in our lives.

## WONDER WOMAN: FEMININE POWER IN ACTION

Wonder Woman is the most popular female superhero of all time. Although she is not the first of the female superheroes, she has remained relevant far longer than most male superheroes. Her origin story also rivals that of any superhero, male or female. Like the Golden Buddha, Wonder Woman was crafted of clay, then imbued with golden gifts on the inside. What makes her unique, in my opinion, is that she truly embodies feminine power. She's not just a female superhero acting like a man, kicking butt and taking names. Wonder Woman is the embodiment of female power that emerges not from deep trauma or loss—as is the case with most superheroes, female or male—but from a deep understanding of who she is as a woman. Even her creation story revolves around feminine power.

Before she was Wonder Woman, she was Diana of Themyscira, princess of the immortal Amazons. The Amazons, a tribe of warrior women, were created around 1200 B.C. when the Greek goddesses drew forth the souls of all women who had been murdered by men and placed them on the island of Themyscira.

One soul, the unborn daughter of the first woman ever murdered by a man, was held back from creation. She would be created in the 20th century when Hippolyta, the queen of the Amazons, was instructed to take clay from the shores of Paradise Island and mold it into a baby girl.

Six members of the Greek Pantheon granted the soul a gift, then bonded the soul to the clay, giving it life. Their soul gifts were superpowers. Demeter gave Diana great strength; Athena, wisdom and courage; Artemis, a hunter's heart and a communion with animals; Aphrodite, beauty and a loving heart; Hestia, sisterhood with fire; Hermes, speed and the power of flight. Diana thus emerged as an incredibly skilled and smart woman, bestowed with amazing offerings from the gods themselves.

But Diana wasn't *just* born a powerful and gifted baby girl. She grew up surrounded by a legion of powerful sisters and mothers. She was trained in the ways of war, but also of peace. Every day of her life prepared her for her destiny.

As Diana entered her teens and early adulthood, the gods ordered

Queen Hippolyta to send a warrior into the world of man. So Hippolyta ordered a contest to be held. However, she forbade Diana from competing. Diana disobeyed and entered the competition in disguise. She easily won the contest and was named the Amazon's champion and the woman who would be sent into the world of men.

Fast forward to the 21st century where we find Diana fighting alongside men in a war to end all wars. Here, she finally discovers her full powers and true destiny. She fights crime and Nazis as a powerful, brave warrior, yet she also favors the pen, diplomatically resolving conflicts with her nurturing and honest attitude. Her creator, William Moulton Marston, designed Wonder Woman to be an "ideal love leader"; as he explained, "Wonder Woman is psychological propaganda for the new type of woman who should, I believe, rule the world."[2] Her popularity has brought her into the 21st century as the titular star of the first female-directed and female-led Hollywood blockbuster in history.

Wonder Woman holds the power of flight, but more importantly, she holds the power of wisdom, beauty, a loving heart, courage, strength, and even the ability to commune with animals. She also has a sisterhood forged in fire and passion. She is more than a fighting machine. She is a creator of life and peace. Thus, it's not hard to understand why Wonder Woman has outlasted most superheroes, male or female. She isn't just a beautiful woman acting like a man. She is both fully female and fully male in her psychic energy.

So Wonder Woman's powers are pretty spectacular, and she is one of our most inspiring fictional heroes. But realistically, what does today's woman have in common with a mythical superhero? Does she actually have anything in common with Wonder Woman? What is a true or real superpower?

Let's look at the six superpowers the gods gave Princess Diana and compare them to what we, as women, have to draw on today:

- **Great strength** – Like Superman, Diana could lift cars, and

---

2    Quoted in Jill Lepore, "The Surprising Origin Story of Wonder Woman," Smithsonian Magazine, October 2014, http://www.smithsonianmag.com/arts-culture/origin-story-wonder-woman-180952710/.

according to her story, could "move one-third of the earth." Her physical strength was necessary, and she used it to support or enhance her other powers. While we may not possess the same physical strength as Wonder Woman, we often underestimate the physical strength we do have, particularly when it comes to childbirth and protection of our loved ones.

- **Wisdom and courage** – She didn't rely solely on muscle. Diana was also strongly intuitive and profoundly confident. Her wisdom and courage included a strong belief in herself and others, something women today can and should tap into whenever possible.

- **Intuition, a hunter's heart and a communion with animals** – The best hunters are intuitive. They put themselves in their quarry's place. They think like them, respond like them, understand them. Don't think that hunting is all about tracking down animals to kill. We also hunt to find food, a safe place to relocate our tribe, and resources and opportunity. Hunting is a skill. To hunt, or find something or someone, we need to know where to look, what the signs are—no matter how subtle and how to capture our prey, be it a job, a career, an opportunity, or a lifestyle.

- **Beauty and a loving heart** – Wonder Woman is certainly a physically beautiful woman, and an eternally beautiful woman at that. But beauty is more than skin deep, as she shows us. It's her compassion and loving heart, her courage and passion for healing, helping, and saving others and, most of all, becoming a force for good, that comprises her real beauty. We would do well to take note of these qualities in ourselves.

- **Sisterhood with fire** – Wonder Woman never acted alone. She was raised by powerful, wise women, and she relied on their wisdom and strength as well as her own. We must do the same. "Fire" in this book is about passion, excitement, determination.

- **Speed and the power of flight** – Speed is more than "going fast." It's about acting decisively, about moving quickly when needed, and waiting patiently when silence is called for. If we watch birds, we'll see that while they may all fly, flight is not what is always called for. There is the Great Blue Heron that stands motionless for hours, poised and focused on his prey, striking at the perfect time. There is the hummingbird, small, but lightning quick, hovering, darting, and yes, resting as needed. Eagles soar, riding on the strength of their wings, not the power of them. They can dive, climb, soar, and strike in flight. Think of the reasons behind the need to fly as well as the act itself.

Women today have, seek, and share many of Diana's superpowers. All of the powers the gods gave Diana, we have as women now. It's our essence, our nature, our energy. While men want to conquer and control, women want to create lives that express who they truly are. They want that expression to be about their gifts—the same gifts Diana had. Women want to realize their higher spiritual potentials, their relationship potential, and their creative abilities including, but also beyond, giving birth. They want to be mothers who create deeper, more meaningful lives. I'd like to highlight five superpowers in particular that we all have as women:

### 1. WISDOM, COURAGE, BELIEF

Of the superpowers that I think we all share, the first is belief, specifically belief in ourselves if we choose to tap into this power. It's not a power that is "faster than the speed of sound," and it won't help us "leap tall buildings in a single bound," but, believing in yourself will help you overcome impossible odds and accomplish great things. A belief in yourself will also help you meet the challenge of tasks and projects no one believes we, as women, can accomplish. It's real.

Both men and women have the ability to believe in things and have faith they can accomplish them. It's certainly not something that's unique to gender. But I will tell you, as I ponder the movies and plays

I've watched or the iconic characters I've loved, I think about the role that the woman has played in believing in something that wasn't possible. Believing in a project, in themselves, or in their child when the odds were very much against them are examples where belief does indeed become a superpower.

When women have believed in the healing of someone they love in spite of a doctor's cautions and claims to the contrary, many have realized the power of their strong beliefs. Or take the examples of women who have believed in their spouses or children, only to hear later, "I believe the only reason I was able to achieve what I did was because of your belief in me."

Your beliefs do matter, for you and for others. When someone feels that another's belief in them pushed them beyond what they thought was possible, that's evidence that you do indeed hold this superpower. This is the never-ending beauty of a loving heart.

Since the beginning of time, women have been the ones who have carried and delivered life. They have nurtured families and raised children in communities around the globe. They are the ones with bundles of intuition, understanding, and knowledge. It's their hormones, wisdom, insight, and ability to give, help, and see others in a way that not only validates the people in their lives but pulls the strength, power, vision, and abilities to the surface.

I think belief is one of women's superpowers. It comes so naturally and easily to us that we don't always recognize how powerful it really is. We're more than cheerleaders and supporters. We're the force that finds the power hidden in others, like the Golden Buddha. We don't see the clay. We don't bemoan the cracks. We look for the sparkle, the small glint of light that flickers under our gaze and searching light, and we run back to the family, the tribe, the people around us and help others see it as well. It's not that we create the gold, but that we see it beneath the dirt and cracks and clay and cobwebs. Where others see filth and failure, women often see potential and hope and a future. And like the monks who spent a dark, stormy night chipping away at the clay, women will spend time chipping away at the armor, fear, and distrust of their vision until the Golden Buddha is revealed.

## 2. INTUITION, A HUNTER'S HEART AND A COMMUNION WITH ANIMALS

"A hunter's heart" is a reference to the ability of someone to connect to the land, to animals, and to the challenge of tracking prey or destiny. This is something that must be nurtured, trained, and honed. This uniquely powerful ability is our greatest superpower. This is what's known as our *intuition*. We've all heard for many, many years—since the beginning of time—that women tend to be very intuitive. It's not just anecdotal; it's scientific. Studies have shown women have better, stronger, and more accurate intuition, at times bordering on what appears to be psychic powers. According to research discussed in *Psychology Today* in 2011, women's intuition exists. Women have the ability to read nonverbal cues better than men, and thus are more likely to notice or intuit the "subtle emotional messages" others send out into the world.[3]

Again, it's not something unique to just women, but it does seem to come more naturally to us. There are countless stories of women intuitively knowing things about their children, families, or loved ones. Wonder Woman regularly relied on her intuition to make decisions and solve crimes for the betterment of humanity.

Our insight comes to us in very subtle inklings and messages throughout the day. We tend to acknowledge these glimmers if it's something really big, but not as often when they nudge us in subtle ways. However, when I listen to Suzie Superstar talking about putting in the work *and* following the little things that keep coming up in her life, I know she is talking about intuition.

When women follow this subtle path—when they turn to one side or another, or make that phone call, or invite a stranger to coffee, or do some simple, seemingly inconsequential step—it turns into the most powerful moment of their lives. They end up being in the right place at the right time to meet the famous director, bump into the love of their lives, or achieve whatever it is they do that changes their life course forever and for the better.

---

3    Ronald E. Riggio, "Women's Intuition: Myth or Reality?," Psychology Today, July 14, 2011. https://www.psychologytoday.com/blog/cutting-edge-leadership/201107/women-s-intuition-myth-or-reality

Our intuition is incredibly powerful. It's not a skill you learn in school. It's not something that's bestowed on you because of a title. It's something you were born with and that you develop. If you listen to it, exercise it, use it, and learn to walk hand in hand with it throughout your life, it becomes a superpower.

Albert Einstein described intuition as "a feeling for the order lying behind the appearance of something." It's incredibly empowering to know that at any time throughout the day, if you could do one or two small things, your life would change. One of those things is to be silent and hear what comes to you. Another, as you're going about your day, start to recognize and listen to those little subtle voices that come to you. Learn to recognize when and when not to act. When you do, life and all its treasures manifest in ways that you can't even imagine.

### 3. NONVIOLENT VERSUS VIOLENT BEHAVIOR

Archeological evidence suggests that there was a time period— maybe 20,000 years ago—when men and women lived as equals. Neither gender was more dominant nor more powerful than the other. The so-called feminine qualities of compassion, nurturing, and nonviolence were equally shared by both men and women.

Men and women were both revered as healers. In spite of what all women shared with men, we were respected for our greater intuitive strengths and our ability to find peace in strife. But, over time, force won out over peace as the main way to resolve conflict. Life evolved so that the physically strongest person was the person who won the argument, got the food, and triumphed over neighboring tribes. It was the stronger warrior, typically men, who learned to rule over their families or within their own tribe by force, not cooperation and collaboration. The intuition, wisdom, and ways of cooperation both men and women shared gave way to "might makes right."

Still, there were many Native American tribes, as well as other communities around the world, where women continued to rule. Women owned the property and made the decisions. Over time, even those tribes gave way, turning from a matriarchal (female) rule to a patriarchal (male) rule.

You often hear—and I think men would acknowledge this, too—that the world would probably be a more peaceful place and we'd have less violence if women were in charge. This is not to advocate for women and oppose men, or to say all women are more peaceful. Many are as consumed with might and power as men. I believe that, in general, it is in women's nature to find ways to create harmony, to create something that works for everyone involved, and to seek mutually beneficial solutions versus giving in to the strongest person in the room.

I don't believe the majority of women are looking to prove their power in terms of strength or in their ability to harm another person in order to win. I believe a woman's nature is healing and more compassionate. Our nature is one that wants to come to a mutual, peaceful agreement versus believing that the answer will come through force and violence.

#### 4. THE ABILITY TO LISTEN TO OUR RESPONSIVE UNIVERSE

There are times when you are silent. This could be during meditation or just simple silence born of listening to the world around you. Your silent moments offer great opportunity to listen to whatever your higher power wants to share with you. There are other times when, as you're going about your day, you start to sense what it feels like to be communicated to by someone or something greater than yourself. During these moments, you understand that this force is acting on your behalf and for your good. This intuition—hearing the right voice, knowing that what you're about to do is right, but not knowing why—that's all part of unlocking the superpower we all have.

Now that I'm back to locks and secrets, I want us all to think about a combination lock that perhaps we had in high school for our hall or gym locker. Can you remember your first combination lock? Likely you don't. But what you may remember about those locks is that when you aligned those numbers correctly, you heard and even felt a little click or vibration. When you heard it or felt it, you always knew, "Okay, I got it." You knew the lock would open, and you automatically tugged at it, knowing it would open. When you didn't hear that little click, then you knew you hadn't used the right number or combination. You had to try again.

Intuition is a lot like that lock. There's a feel, a sound, a vibration to it. What I want you to do is get comfortable with what that little click, that intuitive awareness, sounds like to you. It's so subtle. If you think about it, in a hallway full of high school students, no one but you can really hear your click. Your day is like that crowded hallway. Your hand is on the lock, and only you can sense the click.

As you're going about your day, in the middle of a meeting or your workday, you have to get used to that subtle feeling of intuition. You have to think, "No, stop and do that now." You feel the sensation or something falls into place, and the inkling that came to mind for you pushes you to action. "No, go and do that right now." You don't have to know the whole answer. You don't have to know where it's going to lead, but you begin to know that what you're doing is unlocking something. It's opening you up to the secret, the treasure, the opportunity, or the safety of what's behind your response. "This intuition is a part of my power, and I better follow through or else I lose out on amazing personal insight."

Here's a quick example of how this has worked for me. It was a Sunday. I had the cell phone number of a woman whom I had met at an event that past week who had a significant position with the United Nations. I had her cell number, but I didn't feel like I had the depth of a relationship established that I could call her on the weekends. I was, however, comfortable texting her. She had referred me to a product that I bought and enjoyed, so on a Sunday, after I tried the product, I sent her a simple text saying, "Thank you so much for the referral." I was hesitant to do it because it was a Sunday, but I was feeling so good that I didn't want to wait until Monday. Mostly, I acted because the feeling felt right. It just felt good to me.

So I texted, and her immediate response was "Call me." So I did. We ended up talking for about 45 minutes. Not only did we build a better relationship, but I was then invited to a very exclusive event at the United Nations scheduled for the following month.

The point of my story is that on face value it looks like you have a product – a cream – and you liked it. So what? You thank the person who shared a recommendation to buy it as you might do anytime somebody recommends something to you that you appreciate. The key here is that

## Secret #1: You Have Superpowers

I didn't go back and forth inside my head, second-guessing myself. I also didn't minimize the great feeling of appreciation I developed when her recommendation turned out to be such a good one. Instead, I felt something that told me that I should leverage my feeling and reach out in that moment, and I did. As a result of *trusting my gut,* it led to something far greater than I ever could have imagined: more business and exposure to an opportunity that I have recently been asking for in my life, which is to connect and share my insights with people around the world.

Intuition then is acting on a thought, a feeling. It's that click that goes off in our heads or hearts or both, that tells us that specific moment or thought is powerful. It's not wishful thinking, or random thoughts, hopes, or feelings. Intuition is a sense that comes from an instinctive feeling rather than conscious reasoning. It's not hormones or daydreams. It's specific, like the click on a lock when we've dialed in the right number. It's not spinning the dial and praying the lock opens. It's knowing that it's going to open.

There are other kinds of knowing, things that go beyond taking action on some seemingly random thought or urge. There's the knowledge that we have the power, strength, or ability in the moment—something we wouldn't normally have—that moves us to act.

For instance, think about the mother who lifts a car off of her child. There's no analysis in her mind before or as it happens. There's no *I wonder if I'm going to do it, or if I can do it.* She does it because she's led to do it to save her child. In that situation, it's easier to comprehend. We know how adrenaline works. We know the science behind what makes it possible for a woman to lift a car. We know that most of us would do whatever we can to save our child's life, and insurmountable obstacles suddenly become surmountable when we're energized with our protective instincts and our body's natural response to threat.

We read about these things. We experience some of them. And each time we move through an experience where we should have been shut down or failed, it becomes a lot easier to understand and accept that feeling of intuition. We learn to move forward without a thought, trusting that we'll know what we need to know, when we need to know it. That same superpower is happening all around us, all day every day. It's subtle, but it's there.

If you followed your intuition, you would have those same kinds of experiences that many of us only have a few times in a lifetime. It's possible to tap into that superpower, the one that you tapped into when you lifted the car or the tree off of a child. It's that same superpower and intuition that has led women not to get on planes that later crashed, or attend concerts where a fire, terrorist act, or other tragedy happened. In these cases, we have tapped into some greater, deeper knowledge and wisdom, not because we're super smart or clever, but simply because we've learned to listen.

### 5. PERSONAL VISION AND DREAMS

As we have evolved, we have changed. But inside all of us, there are still these whispered wishes, things deep down that represent our personal vision and our dreams. I love the phrase *whispered wishes* because that's often how they come, quietly but deeply from our gut and connected to our deepest desires.

Depending on the messages you've been receiving in your life or the circumstances that you find yourself in today, you may have disconnected from those wishes. Or you are aware of them, but you just don't believe that they're possible. If it's possible for you to have these visions, it's possible for those things to manifest.

Certainly, there are women who have type A personalities, who know what they want when it comes to their dreams. They go after them; they articulate them; they write them down. You know these women. We see them being honored at their churches, schools, and in our businesses over and over again. Why? Because they absolutely understand their own personal visions and their own dreams.

Then there are many other women who are single moms, who are making it on a limited salary, who are young college students, or who have been abused in some way. They're wondering if their visions are too big or too unrealistic for where they are and who they are. But these visions can't be silenced; they are only ignored. These visions and dreams are always being whispered in our ear when we least expect it. Those whispers are the foundation for your intuition. Those are your dreams that are designed just for you, that your self or soul wants to bring into your life. If you learn to connect with your superpowers, with your intuition, with your visions, you'll be led to the next step in order to manifest those things in your life.

CHAPTER FOUR

# Secret #2: No Super Hero Goes It Alone

No man, or woman, is an island. We've all heard the expression, but many of us don't relate to it. It simply means no one can do it (whatever "it" is) alone. We all need friends, family, connections, and coworkers around us to support, guide, encourage, and work with us if we're going to succeed. Yes, if you are strong and independent, you may say, "I don't need anyone. I'm a one-woman band," but you really haven't thought it through if you're thinking that. We can do a great deal without others, but it's small compared to what we can do with an empowered inner circle of support.

People in general are social creatures. We were created to interact with and need each other. But women are perhaps even more social than men. We had to be to survive, nurture, and care for our families. In a world where everything is digital, global, and automated, we still need those intimate and close connections. This chapter is about why we need to find, create, and maintain those connections, and how we do so. We're not in preschool anymore. Our mothers can't set up play dates for us. We've got to reach out and learn how to connect and nurture sustaining relationships.

## THE SMALL GROUP VERSUS THE LARGE MASSES

What many are experiencing today is the loss of both our small group and larger community connections. Never before has it been so important to connect to individuals with whom you can share deeply and grow from your sharing. Last year, Dr. Oz identified this situation as a growing epidemic of loneliness. This affliction affects women in particular. According to a survey Dr. Oz conducted with over 1,500 women across the country, 60% of the respondents say they deal with loneliness and 20% of them say they are lonely most of the time.[4]

What can you do to stop the spread of disconnection? How can you build a support network that feeds your mind and spirit while also helping you reach your goals faster and more completely? Start with looking at your current relationships.

### ASSESS YOUR RELATIONSHIPS

Below is an assessment from the top-selling book *Making Your Net Work: The Art and Science of Career and Business Networking* by authors Billy Dexter, a partner in Diversity at the top executive search firm Heidrick and Struggles, and Melissa G. Wilson, co-creator of the award-winning process of "Networlding," along with Jocelyn Carter Miller, the first Chief Marketing Officer of Motorola.

This form will help you pinpoint what you can do to network better, where the weak spots in your networking skills are, and ways to change and act to make your networking more authentic and helpful.

### YOUR TURN: TAKE THE "MAKING YOUR NET WORK" ASSESSMENT

Put a mark in the square that best represents your response to each statement. No one will see this but you, so be honest with yourself.

---

4    http://www.foxbusiness.com/features/2016/10/06/dr-oz-have-loneliness-epidemic.html.

# Secret #2: No Super Hero Goes It Alone

| Score | Never = 1 | Seldom = 2 | Sometimes = 3 | Often = 4 | Always = 5 |
|---|---|---|---|---|---|
| I believe it's important to make a difference. | | | | | |
| I believe anything is possible. | | | | | |
| I believe I am guided by strong inner beliefs, intent, or principles. | | | | | |
| I believe in partnering with others. | | | | | |
| I believe that with great networking partners I can get powerful results. | | | | | |
| I believe people are my most creative resource. | | | | | |
| I share my goals with my networking partners. | | | | | |
| I build and nurture relationships with my networking partners. | | | | | |

| Score | Never = 1 | Seldom = 2 | Sometimes = 3 | Often = 4 | Always = 5 |
|---|---|---|---|---|---|
| I limit relationships with selfish individuals and those who don't help me realize my goals. | | | | | |
| I respect the creative process of networking. | | | | | |
| I believe that good networking shortens the time it takes to achieve my goals. | | | | | |
| I assume that good networking is a balanced process of giving and asking for support. | | | | | |
| I believe that good networking can help me achieve most of my goals. | | | | | |
| When networking, I ask for what I need and/or want. | | | | | |

# Secret #2: No Super Hero Goes It Alone

| Score | Never = 1 | Seldom = 2 | Sometimes = 3 | Often = 4 | Always = 5 |
|---|---|---|---|---|---|
| When networking, I work to discover the interests and needs of those with whom I network. | | | | | |
| When networking, I expect to discover/create new opportunities for me and my networking partners. | | | | | |
| I network with people who can make introductions regularly. | | | | | |
| I offer emotional support, information, and other support to my networking partners. | | | | | |
| I respond quickly to the requests and needs of my networking partners. | | | | | |
| I measure the results of networking efforts. | | | | | |

Total your score. Retake this quiz periodically to see how you change, or if you change. Again, you are the only one who will see the results, so be honest with yourself.

Building an empowered inner circle starts with the understanding that no one, not even a superhero, goes it alone. We all need, can, and should connect with others as collaborators and, therefore, accelerators of our respective and collective goals.

Let's say, for example, you want to create a powerful community initiative that will address ongoing issues around (put your cause du jour here) where you live. You start by turning to people you already know, realizing that those you know have at least 10 key people in their respective networks you very well may not have met ... yet. It's a fact. We are all busy, and we can't keep up with everything going on in our friends' lives. So, the good news here is that we can now invite our friends to invite their friends to a gathering, where we can get their support for our cause.

## CREATE AN INFRASTRUCTURE TO CREATE MEANINGFUL CONNECTIONS

I'm not at a loss for *where* I can meet people. But sometimes I struggle with the *mental space* necessary to forge meaningful connections.

Let's say I have just come back from two weeks of business travel. My home is a mess, I need to get my hair done, I need to pay my bills, etc. But I also want to meet up with my boyfriend. Instead of looking forward to meeting him for a drink, it feels like a burden. It's not that he is the burden, but I feel a desire to see him when I'm at my best. And right now, I'm not.

I'm tired, stressed, and feeling undesirable. It's one thing to have a friend who understands me at my worst and knows enough to accept me when I'm a mess, but it's another to have someone I love and want to engage with more intimately. With him, I want to feel strong enough to be there in a positive way. I don't want to see my boyfriend because I'm feeling overwhelmed. I know it will take more of my energy to be fully present and focused during our time together. Anything I do that requires even the tiniest little extra energy is just another burden.

If you have experienced similar frustrations, here are some tips to create more space for connection:

- **Make it simple.** It's like physical therapy. You don't bounce back after surgery immediately, but rather slowly and deliberately, over time. Just start with something simple like getting together for coffee rather than trying to make a full night of something like dinner and a movie.

- **Make it fun.** Build energy that lifts you from a *have to do it* to a *get to do it* mode. Make a game out of those have to's. If you're attending a networking event that you're dreading, tell yourself you'll only introduce yourself to people wearing purple, or to men wearing bowties, or to redheads. Then stick to it. How did you do?

- **Make it a certainty.** Your commitment is to you, the most important person in your life. So, stay steady on your commitment. Don't waver. Any change feels uncomfortable, at first, but with practice, you will eventually turn that effort into something that is effort**less**.

**Steps:**

1. **Create a manifesto on your commitment.** You can do this yourself or you can go to my website www.theerikawalker.com and pull down a manifesto template that I've created for this purpose.

2. **Schedule your first support partner meeting.** However you schedule things (e.g., phone, computer calendar, or old school paper calendar), set your first session with just one support partner. Remember you don't want to overwhelm yourself with new commitments.

3. **Start with an authentic request.** This is about being vulnerable and sharing deeply from your heart. For example, you may say, "I need this more than you may know." Or "What I need help with is holding me accountable or calling me out if I'm disappearing again." Then it's about asking how you can help them.

4. **Ponder How You Can Co-Create.** Once you realize that you don't have to "go it alone," but rather, you can *co-create* opportunities with others who hold similar values, you will be able to accomplish goals in half the time it takes you to go it alone.

5. **Set up follow-up meetings.** By putting a next connection date on your respective calendars, you both will better continue on the momentum of support you shared during your first exchange.

**Example:**

Carol, a shy introvert, hated networking. She saw it as a chore, as fake, as something people did in order to justify using each other. She told her boss as much, but was still assigned to the week-long annual conference held out of town. Not only would she be among thousands of strangers, she'd be in a new city where she didn't know how to get around. She was explaining all this to her best friend Liz, a raging extrovert.

"I wish I could go with you," Liz said. "It sounds like a dream week."

"For you, maybe," Carol said. "Not for me. My boss thinks it will help me be less introverted, but that's not how introversion works." She sighed.

"Hey, it's perfect," Liz said. "You like one-on-one stuff, right?"

Carol nodded as she kept packing her suitcase.

"Let's create a special sign for you then. Rather than be at this conference, what would you prefer to be doing?"

Carol thought about it.

"I'd rather be sitting on the beach, drinking wine, and petting my cat," she said.

"Perfect."

The next day, Liz picked her up to take her to the airport and handed her a necklace with a dish saucer sized sign, like a pendant. The sign had a cartoon drawing of a cat stretched out next to a bottle and a glass of wine with the words, "I'd rather be on the beach drinking wine and petting my cat. Introduce yourself if you feel the same." Carol laughed out loud and said, "I can't wear that!"

"Why not?" Liz said. "What have you got to lose?"

Carol thought about it for a minute. "You're right," she said. "I'll do it."

For the next five days, Carol wore the sign. The reactions surprised her. Many people laughed and shared what they would rather be doing than attending the conference. The conversations she had were authentic, fun, and energizing as she got to do what she loved best – listen to others talk. There was no pressure to "make" small talk, as people were excited about what they'd rather be doing. Many pressed their business cards into her hands and asked for hers.

While hundreds of people stopped to share, about a dozen or so stopped to say, "OMG, I wish I were at the beach, drinking wine and petting my cat, too!" Carol suddenly realized she shared her dream with a lot of people, one of whom was one of the conference organizers!

By the time the conference was over, Carol was regretting that it had to end. She had had dinner with several of her fellow cat and wine people, made several business deals, and had become known as "the cat lady" to most of the conference attendees. The conference organizers mentioned her "brilliant" networking idea at the closing dinner, and one even said he'd emailed her boss with a photo of her surrounded by people.

Networking, she realized, doesn't have to be dull.

"I owe you big time," she told her friend Liz as she loaded her bags into Liz's car once she was home. "It was amazing."

What Liz knew and Carol learned was that the best networking is authentic, fun, simple, and real. People connect over shared interests. Liz simply found a way to make that interest quickly visible. Once Carol was back at work, it was easy for her to reach out to people with a "Hello again from the Cat Lady" in her email subject line. People immediately recognized her nickname and opened the email. Carol was able to send photos and start a business relationship with many of the people whose cards and companies interested her.

It's not just Liz and Carol who learned that people like to talk about their interests. The organizers of the TED talks do, too. They don't use big signs, but on the name tags they issue attendees, they ask the person to list the three most passionate topics they like to talk about on their name tag. So, it's not unusual to see a marine biologist with a name tag that says "Michael" with "Narwhals, Mermaids, and Pirates" under his name; or a venture capitalist named Tom with "30-Second Elevator Talks, Passion, and Great Stories" under his.

When we look for the things we have in common, people we enjoy talking to, and the interests we share rather than money-making opportunities, the networking takes care of itself.

After hearing about Carol's story, her friend Todd, also an introvert, went out and had a t-shirt made. On the front and back it read, "Introvert. I love Thai food, documentary movies, and long silent pauses. Please introduce yourself if you do, too."

He began wearing the shirt everywhere – when he ran, at the gym, in the park walking his dog, and at parties. In less than six months, he met the woman Anna, an extrovert that he would later marry. "She was so beautiful and perfect, I would never have introduced myself," he told me. "She saw my shirt and laughed and laughed and came over and introduced herself. We clicked immediately. Our first date was Thai food and a movie documentary about travel. She travels a lot for her job and wanted me to see some of the places she'd been."

Turning yourself into a human billboard isn't new. We have all worn shirts with our favorite sports teams, bands, or other interests to tell the world what we like. Carol and Todd just took it a step further with an invitation to connect. And that's what networking is – connection.

If you're not a t-shirt or sign-wearing type, you can do the same with your wardrobe, jewelry, bag, or purse. Find something you love, and use it to stand out and let people know what you like.

Another friend of mine is fascinated by brooches and pins because her grandmother wore a different one every day. She networks by finding women with brooches and expressing interest in the pin, asking about the story behind it while sharing her story about her grandmother's most beautiful or funny pins. The resulting conversations often end up moving to a coffee shop or lunch, and a networking connection.

Learn to look. Learn to listen. There is always a connection to be found if you take time to see people as human beings with interests, and not just as potential business deals.

# CHAPTER FIVE

# Secret #3: Deliberately Create Your Reality

Deliberate creation of reality means that you can literally create anything in your physical life that you can envision in your mental life. If you can see it, feel it, and project it, you can manifest it. You can be, do, and have anything you want, depending on your spiritual background or if you're heavy into the law of attraction or positive thinking, of course. You've heard some things like that before. But don't roll your eyes just yet. These tactics and methods of creating our reality have now been proven by science.

I want to lay that foundation of fact first. As we move forward, I want you to know this concept of being able to really create anything is real. It works. And now, let's look at the background and science of how that's actually possible.

Everything in the universe is made from a quantum field. The study of this is called theoretical physics, or quantum field theory (QFT). The quantum field is an invisible field of energy that represents all possibilities. Every single thing you see – whether it's a dog, cat, good relationship, not so good a relationship, a penny, or a $100 bill – is all made up of the same four basic elements: hydrogen, oxygen, nitrogen, and carbon.

For example, the only difference between a penny and a $100 bill, or a dog and a chair, is how those different elements are combined and the rate of speed at which they're vibrating. It's almost too simple, right? Only it's not. The power is *in* the simplicity.

It's important that you know that you're really a powerful creator, and the elements that make up reality are elements available to all of us. The only thing that shapes our reality or the matter that we create has to do with us. From the Buddha to Christ, the truth is that "As a (wo) man thinks, so they are." Every enlightened and powerful teacher since the beginning of time has taught this concept. So why do so few believe it? Because until recently there was no real science to back up what so many have known and experienced—that we actually do create our own reality.

It's all about the vibrations you are holding and therefore, giving to others. When I say the word "vibration," I mean that your life holds a vibrating energy. It's electromagnetic. That means that life is attracting like things to itself. Have you ever struck and held two tuning forks up to each other? They will either begin to vibrate at the same frequency, or one will cancel the other out and both will stop vibrating. Physicians use tuning forks to diagnose many medical conditions. Tuning forks are used to test vibration sense throughout the body, to evaluate conductive versus neurological hearing loss, and may even be placed under warm or cold water, dried off, and then utilized for temperature sensation evaluation.

One of the most potent examples of the power of vibration is what happens during a large earthquake. The vibrations of the quake can and do liquefy solid earth, swallowing up cars, buildings, and even people.[5] Scientists aren't entirely sure how it works, but they have theories. The one constant through all their theories is vibration.

In this example, like attracts like. This rule applies to your daily life as well. That means that dwelling on certain thoughts will tune those vibrations to you emotionally, spiritually, and mentally, and thus those thoughts will emerge more frequently in your life. They're being manifested to you. The expectations that you have, conscious or not, are literally creating the matter and life that you see before you. When I say that you can create anything, I mean you can create anything. We've got to start dealing with, and being conscious of and responsible for, the

---

5   http://www.sciencemag.org/news/2014/03/how-earthquakes-turn-ground-soup

thoughts that we're thinking and the expectations that we have for who we are as women.

A friend I knew in college, I'll call her Suzanna, was a beautiful, talented, intelligent woman. When I would throw parties for the powerful people in my life, Suzanna was one of the "up and comers" I usually invited. She had a knack for attracting other beautiful, intelligent, talented, and powerful people who could have easily brought her into their circle of influence. However, although she could attract them, it was for only a brief time. They would drift into her life and then quickly move out of it, almost as though repelled like two magnets facing each other.

When I asked some of those people later about what they thought of her, they couldn't quite put their finger on why they weren't interested in pursuing a friendship or business partnership. She was pleasant and appealing enough on the outside, but their repulsion went deeper to their subconscious level. "We just didn't click like I thought we would" was a typical response I got. I understood. What I knew that they didn't know was that they and Suzanna looked similar and were similar in some ways, but at their core, they were vibrating on different levels.

I soon learned Suzanna's personal life was filled with men and women who used, abused, and disrespected her. Her relationships were a disaster. She was constantly getting involved with, then abandoned by, masculine alpha males who turned out to be homosexuals struggling with their sexuality. After college, Suzanna admitted she, too, was struggling with her own sexuality. Her vibrations around the uncertainty with who she was were attracting like-minded vibrations in the men she was attracted to.

When we are needy, lonely, and insecure, we attract other people who are also lonely, needy, and insecure. They may not appear to be that way at first, but in time, if we look closely enough, we discover how much we truly do have in common. Suzanna got into therapy and began to examine and change some thought patterns in her life. When she did, she noticed she was no longer attracting, or being attracted to, the kinds of men and people she used to cling to. Her vibration levels were changing. She began to meet like-minded women who shared her interests and sexual preference.

There's an old method many therapists use to get to know their clients quickly. They ask them about their friends. They know that the people, circumstances, and events in our lives mirror who we are and what we think about ourselves. Looking at the physical state of a person's friends, job, surroundings, and life is a very accurate predictor of what's happening vibrationally inside of them.

As much as we try to hide, disguise, or ignore who we are and at what level we vibrate, it's impossible. The only way to change your vibration is to opt for positive versus negative thoughts. What most people do, however, is create an ongoing tug of war with themselves when they say what they want in one breath and then say what they don't want in the next. This, as Esther Hicks, an expert on how our thoughts turn to things (good or bad) shares, is what keeps us from having what we *want*. Stay with your focus on what you want and stay steadily focused on that. From this vantage point of positive focus, you will move toward those things that, up until now, have been eluding you. For those of you who want to take a deep dive into what Esther refers to as "The Art of Allowing," go to YouTube and start watching her many videos that are free.

### FENG SHUI

Physical spaces and things have an energy and vibration of their own, just like we do. Their energy and vibration, like ours, can be manipulated and changed. When someone who works with energy and vibration, such as a Shaman, wants to change something, she calls upon different frequencies to physically shift those vibrations and move that energy on a molecular level. She creates a specific vibration. You may not be able to mentally or emotionally do this yet, at least not consciously, but you can do it physically.

Try this. Do you have a cluttered home? A cluttered car? A cluttered closet? Clean them. I mean be ruthless. Get the clutter out, throw away the trash, give away items you aren't wearing anymore. Do a big clean. Wash it down, make it shine. Now, keep that space clean for a week and see if things don't begin to change.

First of all, you'll feel the different vibration when you walk into the space as soon as it's been cleaned. Remember how I said objects, whether a dog or a $100 bill, have vibrations, too? What you're feeling is a change in the vibration of that space because you've physically changed the objects in relation to one another, and thus the vibrations have shifted.

Now, start watching to see what else happens. You'll be amazed. What you have done is shift the vibrations. You've begun to align the vibration of your energy with the vibration of something higher, causing you to feel better. When you release lower vibrations – or negative beliefs – which hold you down and block you from aligning with what you want, you attract higher vibrations. Everything in your reality is a reflection of your vibration. The people you meet, the job opportunities you have or don't have, the house you live in, the friends you have, even the mood you're in, are all a mirror that's reflecting what is going on inside of you.

It doesn't take a lot to shift your vibration. Feng Shui does this through something as simple as putting fresh flowers in a certain part of the room, or moving furniture to a new space, or even turning your bed to face another part of the room. There are other ways to shift your vibration, but physically changing your environment is a fast, quick way to see how it works.

If you want to examine your own vibrational level, look at your past. Many times, our expectations are borne out of our prior experiences. That's normal. Because they come from these experiences, they're what I like to call our observations.

Day to day, we see different things. Day to day, we are reflecting on experiences that we've had. Many times, those two things combine and create our expectations, typically on an unconscious level. Meaning, we're creating our life without even realizing it. We see a lot of negative or scary items on the news, and we start to expect that perhaps those events could happen to us. We are surrounded by people who have great marriages, and our friends have great marriages, and we are in an environment – maybe a church or something – with great marriages, and we sort of start to expect that our marriage can be great, too. We change our vibration and begin to open up to higher vibrations or lower ones, depending on what we create for ourselves.

The key is to create the life you want, not just the life your current subconscious wants, and we do this through being mindful. You need to be an observer of your own thoughts so that you can start to see what happens when you are expecting things on a conscious level – or I'll say deliberately – in favor of what you want. You'll also begin to see when you unconsciously expect things you don't want because you aren't conscious of the things that you're observing and thinking about all of the time.

Something to be aware of is that you can only attract what you believe you deserve. Even if you attract what you want, if you don't believe you deserve it, it will quickly flee or fade. Remember Suzanna, who was initially able to attract wealthy, intelligent, and powerful people to her at social gatherings, but unable to turn that attraction into something that lasted.

The direction and the excitement here is that every day you have an opportunity to think about what it is that you really desire and things that are connected to that desire. You can feel what it's like to have it and allow that to become an expectation for you in your life. As you believe it, you will see it manifest before your eyes.

I'll give you a tool that can help you understand how that works. I like to use some of the teachings from Neville Goddard. He has this philosophy called "Feel it real." What that means is as you think about something that you want, you should not only think about it, but consider it from the perspective of it already happening.

As an example, if I want a shiny new Mercedes, I would not only think about the Mercedes, but I would also visualize going to my best friend's house, driving up her driveway, and seeing her exclaim, "Erika, that's a beautiful car!" I visualize myself being excited about what is happening and *how it makes me feel.* What that says to my vibrational state is that it has already happened. My mind doesn't know the difference between what has happened and what's going to happen. We've got this field that we talked about – this quantum field of possibilities. It doesn't make any decisions for us. We're the decision-makers here.

If we are pulling out that energy that says, "It's already done because I already had this congratulatory conversation from my best friend about how beautiful my car is," then I have put that energy out into that field, and I can expect to see it. I know I can expect to see it.

I want to give you a couple of stories from my own life and my experiences with friends and colleagues.

## Secret #3: Deliberately Create Your Reality

Here's the first. I was coaching a woman I'll call Elizabeth. She was an entrepreneur, but her business wasn't going that well. She decided that she wanted a consistent income in an environment that would be really fun for her, where she could learn and also teach other people. That was her focus.

She got to a point where she was just ecstatic about that being her reality. I mean ecstatic. She called me one day and said, "I absolutely know that I can have any position that I want inside of an organization or with my own business." This is a person who had been in a corporate environment. She knew what it felt like to be where she was seeing herself being.

Shortly after that call, a headhunter contacted her about a human resources position at a college. Now, she had not been in higher education at all except for her own schooling. She went for the interview for the Vice President of Human Resources for a prominent college. She had the interview, and she said the person who interviewed her – who was the President of the college – did not show any emotion, didn't seem overly happy about the interview, and saw there were gaps in my client's resume and skills that she knew she really didn't have. She is a solid HR professional, but there were certainly gaps in terms of the educational background.

But she said to me, "It doesn't matter. I'm going to get this position. I already know it. I can already feel it." She told me about seeing herself come into the school as an employee. She saw one of the people who happened to be really nice to her during the interview process telling her, "Welcome. We're so glad to have you."

Within three days of her interview, Elizabeth was offered a contract for this position.

We were both elated about the offer. She worked with them for a couple of months and then they told her very clearly, "This is a contract position until we find a permanent person because it takes a long time to get a permanent person in higher ed." After a couple of months, she said, "I think I want this full time." But the rule was the contract she signed said you cannot go from contractor to full-time employee.

Well, lo and behold, give it another 30 days or so, and they offered her the full-time position even though she had signed a contract to the contrary. She was there for a couple of years and then decided to transition and do something else.

I say all that to show how she was *feeling it real.* She could not only visualize what it looked like in the end to have that new person congratulate or welcome her to this new job, she could *feel* it. Even before that position she could feel that she could have any leadership role that she wanted to, no matter what the company or the environment was. After the interview, she happened to go by the desk where she'd be working. She'd already seen the pictures there on the wall and knew in her mind how it was going to be decorated.

The *feeling it* step is a step above what you may be familiar with in terms of visualization. This looks like imagining what it actually would feel like once you realize the manifestation of your dream or vision. This involves you putting out a focused vibration around your intention into that quantum field. You are essentially telling the world that you have realized your vision. Now going about your life in the manner that you would once something that you want has been completed.

The purpose of explaining the science behind this phenomenon is so that as you read the pages in this book, you understand how powerful you really are. As you're in your own personal environment and you think about where you want to be as a woman in the workplace, your first responsibility is to embrace the power that you have. Don't be distracted and sucked into what's there now. For instance, an acquaintance of mine named Alice began her career in what was essentially an office pool of administrators. If someone's assistant was sick, or on leave, or if they needed a temp, they would call on this pool of men and women to fill in briefly. Once their assignment for that day or week or month was over they went from their higher position back to "the pool."

Alice decided early on, after working for a couple of days for the CEO, that she didn't want to go back to the pool after every assignment. She envisioned herself being transferred to other executives, bypassing the pool. This wasn't how things were done, but somehow it was how things began to work for her. Instead of being sent back to file, type, and do menial administrative tasks, CEOs began to depend on her and move her around until finally one of them (the one she saw herself working with) hired her permanently. It happened because she stopped focusing on being "in the pool" and all that that meant, and started focusing on where she ultimately wanted to be.

If you are currently making less or you're currently in a role that you don't particularly care for, you might find that you do as many of us do – automatically dwell on that and dwell on all of the experiences that are connected to that. Because of this electromagnetic field, we're actually strengthening that vibration and drawing more of those negative experiences to us instead of what we really want.

I know it's easier to dwell on what you see and experience every day. I know that you've had some experiences that are not great. I know that there are lots of statistics and facts about why you can and cannot move to the next role, level, or organization. I'm going to challenge you to ignore all of it. It exists, but it's in flux. None of those rules, policies, or experiences trump how the universe was actually created.

You have to understand your own power and get very disciplined in thinking about what it is that you want. When you do, you also have to learn to *expect* those things to show up.

I want everyone who reads this to understand and believe that all matter is simply vibrating energy that can be changed. I want you to know that your expectations, your creation of that vibrating energy can, will, and does manifest itself in some form. By some form, I mean your reality is based on your feelings. You get what you expect. You become what you think you are or what you deserve.

Your reality starts with a thought, but your thought then leads to a feeling. What really gets the energy going at a particular rate, making it even more pronounced in this energy field, comes from your feelings. Your feelings don't just happen. Good or bad, positive or negative, they are directly related to a specific, particular thought. If you're thinking that a particular experience is a bad one, then your feelings will be similar, and that energy will be stronger around whatever those feelings are.

Conversely, if you don't label something as bad – or you consciously label it as good – then it allows you to have a more positive energy or more positive feelings about what it is that you actually want, or whatever it is that you're focused on.

What's so important about this is, whether you believe it or not, it's happening. And it's happening every second of the day whether you decide to change it or not. That doesn't mean you have to be paranoid. We all have around 40,000 thoughts every day. You can't worry and then think, "Oh, I had a negative thought in that moment." It probably is not going to attract anything because it doesn't have any momentum. It doesn't have any feeling unless you choose to dwell on it and feed it that energy.

We do have to be concerned about our repetitive thoughts. Those repetitive thoughts are usually ones we're not conscious of, so we're unconsciously creating. All those subconscious thoughts about our unworthiness, of our not being loveable, all that baggage from childhood and our past is there quietly feeding those repetitive vibrations of lack, of negativity.

We've also got to be conscious of those thoughts that we have strong feelings about, especially if they're not good ones because we're also creating in those moments.

Many times, we like to say, "I have a right to feel bad, or angry, or vengeful. I got fired. Of course I'm going to be sad. Of course I'm going to be in fear." Or "This person left me. I have a right to be sad. I have a right to be upset. I have a right to feel rejected, less than, unlovable." Or "This person stole my money. Of course I'm upset."

It doesn't mean that you don't have some human feelings about what's happening to you, but it does mean that you have to monitor how long you allow those feelings to go on. Think of yourself in a small, airtight room. Your feelings are a fire hose of water pouring into that room. Letting that water (emotions) pour in and getting your feet wet is one thing, but letting the water fill up the room until you drown is quite another.

You're going to have to tell yourself a different story. Even if you were fired or this person left you or whatever, it doesn't mean that you can't be sad, but you can also reframe what has happened and tell a more positive story. For example, "Losing that job must mean something else is opening for a new position that I really want." Or "If I totally love this guy, that means that someone even better must be coming." Or "Losing this woman must mean that a much better woman is coming into my life."

If you are certain that you want that person back, then I suggest you focus on all the positive qualities about them. Don't focus on the thought "Oh, my God. They left." Not "I can't believe they've done $X$." Focus on all those positive qualities about that person. Either they will come back or someone with those qualities, or even better qualities, will show up. That is the law of attraction.

We shed millions of cells every day. Our skin, our organs, our hair, our entire self is replaced with new cells every day. We don't grieve the loss of old cells. We don't even think about it. It's just part of life. Snakes shed their skin. Birds molt their feathers. Trees lose their leaves – all in the cycle of something better. Think of your job, friends, relationships, career, opportunities as shedding the old to make way for the new and improved! When you learn to see all of life falling away as a sign that something bigger and better is happening, it will.

If you start doing this today, you'll quickly see results. They may be small. They may not manifest within 24 hours, but that vibration will kickstart something that will show up.

Becky, a freelancer I know, was struggling with paying bills and getting work. She started visualizing and expecting checks in the mail. She was expecting one or two checks, so she decided to visualize getting a check every day for a month. What happened next convinced her that vibrations work. She started visualizing on a Saturday. On Monday, she got a rebate check for $10. The next day she got a payment from a client for $157 that she didn't even know she was owed. It turned out the client she had worked with on the project submitted an invoice for her three months prior.

The next day, she received a $450 check from an affiliate site she'd belonged to for three years but had never had a sale from.

Whether it was a $5 check, or a $500 check, she got checks every day for the rest of the month. Then the random out-of-the-blue checks stopped, but the client checks started. Work began to come in, and her financial fears went away. That's what happens.

As you do these exercises every day, keep in mind that you can always change the vibrations to suit different needs. You always have the freedom to recreate what you had the day before or do something totally different. Also, pay attention to your feelings as to how it progresses and what the feelings are. Think about gauging these feelings on a scale from one to five.

People who experience success with these exercises say that when you do gauge them on a scale from one to five, it's actually even more accurate. A one might be that you're not really feeling it, but you put it down anyway. A five might mean that your whole body is vibrating you feel it so much! Check it every day. Put "I'm at a two today," or "I'm at a three today." Or "I'm at a four." See if you can get up to a level five feeling by the seventh day.

Of course, the other point is that if that works, you do the above for another seven days. Then you do it for another seven days, and you continue to build from your mind to your heart to your actions what you're choosing. You are the creator.

If you've gotten this far and you're still feeling skeptical and thinking this is so far out there it's crazy, then I invite you to try this exercise. Think about something small. Visualize it coming to reality in your life. Stay with this visualization. Share this exercise with friends you think will be open to the process. See what happens.

There is something called empirical evidence. Your experience over time and then the experiences of others over time. This will become your personal scientific foundation. What if you try it and nothing happens? Does that mean this doesn't work? Not necessarily. Rather, it usually means something else is at play here.

We've all seen television commercials for new drugs. When we see one that addresses something we have, we get excited and can't wait to try it. But then the narrator on the commercial says, "Side effects can cause heart attack, numbness, stroke, and death." You don't want the scaly skin that the drug can treat, but what you might get if you take it is a heart attack, death, convulsions, etc. I'm thinking, "I'll stick with my scaly skin, thank you. It's not nearly as bad as a heart attack, stroke, or death."

However, if you look at that commercial, you realize that the majority of the time, this specific drug works. However, there are times when tragedy can strike. It might just be a 1% chance, but the company is legally responsible to tell you what could happen. It's as if someone pointed out how fun it is to run and play in the rain, but then said, "Lightning can strike you and fry you like an overdone egg if you play in the rain."

Sure, this could happen, but the odds are it won't. It's just like someone you love saying, "I think you're the most wonderful person in the world, *but* … ," and the word "but" changes everything. That "but," that 1% negative outcome, ends up having you wipe out all the positive potential of that sentence. This is what happens when you doubt.

There are two points here. First, science is where you see the majority of times X or Y works. In the very beginning of this chapter, I told you that there is scientific evidence for creation and how you can have deliberate creation. I'm asking you to set aside your doubts and trust the science of this. Trust what both medical and psychological researchers and physicists are telling us – this works. Pretend you have no doubts. It's just for one simple exercise. Then you can go back to believing what you want, or not.

Second point: people tend to focus on the negative or bad outcome even if the chance of a negative result is less than 10%. They do this even when the chances of success are overwhelming. We have become a society seeking guarantees rather than a society taking calculated risks.

I promise you this exercise will actually help you experiencing new and better things. From our experiences and those of others – perhaps your spouse, significant other, friends, or family – you will swap stories and start to validate what is happening. You become the scientist. You become the one testing the hypothesis.

I'm not asking you to trust me. I'm asking you to trust the process, to experiment for yourself, and to see if it works or not. But do it. Don't take something for granted. In this case, it's not a drug. It won't hurt you to test this out. The invitation is there to do so and keep an open mind.

That's what I've done through the years as I've changed my own vibrations and my own reality. I know it works. I watch, I look, I assess, and I seek patterns. Actually, because I'm positive, I'm waiting for validation, but I am also open to looking and saying, "What's not working, and why isn't it working?"

What you're doing is finding empirical data/evidence to give proof to the claim that you've seen this work in real life. Your experimentation ends up turning into a tool that you can actually implement on a regular basis.

There is a saying that I love and believe is true as well: "The only thing we can control is our attitude and our actions." In this case, you can decide which attitude you're going to take regarding this exercise and practice. You get to decide that what you're saying is either going to make a difference or not. Either way, that attitude will bubble up through your emotions and change your reality in the way you've decided.

This ability to change reality via shifts in emotion and attitude is also a fact of life. It has been validated through the study and science of emotional intelligence (EQ). Our emotional state is a form of intelligence. Howard Gardner, an American developmental psychologist and the John H. and Elisabeth A. Hobbs Professor of Cognition and Education at the Harvard Graduate School of Education, writes about EQ and intelligence in general. He says there are 22 different forms of intelligence and that all of them play a role in determining our life path. Emotional intelligence is one of them.

Furthermore, Daniel Goleman has shown that emotional intelligence is a better predictive indicator of success than IQ. Goleman is an internationally known psychologist who lectures frequently to professional groups, business audiences, and students and professors on college campuses. As a science journalist, Goleman has reported on the brain and behavioral sciences for the *New York Times* for many years. His 1995 book, *Emotional Intelligence*, was on the *New York Times* bestseller list for eighteen months, with more than 5,000,000 copies published in 40 languages, and it has been a bestseller in many countries. Apart from his books on emotional intelligence, Goleman has written books on topics including self-deception, creativity, transparency, meditation, social and emotional learning, ecoliteracy, and the ecological crisis. He clearly has a lot to say about EQ.

According to his research, "The abilities that set stars apart from the average at work cover the emotional intelligence spectrum: self-awareness, self-management, empathy, and social effectiveness. Both grit and cognitive control exemplify self-management, a key part of emotional intelligence.

"IQ and technical skills matter, of course: they are crucial *threshold* abilities, what you need to get the job done. But everyone you compete with at work has those same skill sets.

"It's the ***distinguishing*** competencies that are the crucial factor in workplace success: the variables that you find only in the star performers

– and those are largely due to emotional intelligence.

"These human skills include, for instance, confidence, striving for goals despite setbacks, staying cool under pressure, harmony and collaboration, persuasion and influence. Those are the competencies companies use to identify their star performers about twice as often as do purely cognitive skills (IQ or technical abilities) for jobs of all kinds.

"The higher you go up the ladder, the more emotional intelligence matters: for top leadership positions they are about 80 to 90 percent of distinguishing competences."[6]

EQ, the emotional quotient, is thus a better predictor of success than IQ. The soft skills required to cultivate emotional intelligence are actually the harder ones to adopt.

Whether you call it a soft science, a spiritual practice, an awareness, or a psychological tool, the fact is vibrations, feelings, emotions, and visualization work.

---

6   Goleman, "What Predicts Success? It's Not Your IQ," published July 17, 2014, http://www.danielgoleman.info/daniel-goleman-what-predicts-success-its-not-your-iq/.

## Exercise

1. Get a notebook and pen. The act of writing something down versus typing it into a computer changes your brain waves and your vibration. Trust me on this.[7]

2. Every morning before you start your day, write down the 10 things you choose to have happen today. Visualize them.

3. As you visualize them, feel them.

4. Write down how strongly you were able to feel them on a scale of 1 to 5.

5. At the end of the week, go back and check off all the things that happened, and make a note about how it happened and how it made you feel.

If you aren't convinced that this process works, then you can walk away, knowing you tried it. But if it does work, then keep doing it and watch your life change!

---

7  http://lifehacker.com/5738093/why-you-learn-more-effectively-by-writing-than-typing; http://www.npr.org/2016/04/17/474525392/attention-students-put-your-laptops-away; http://www.medicaldaily.com/why-using-pen-and-paper-not-laptops-boosts-memory-writing-notes-helps-recall-concepts-ability-268770

CHAPTER SIX

# Secret #4: It's Not The Spoon That Bends; It's You

*"It's not the circumstances that change, it's you." ~ The Matrix*

I love *The Matrix* movies. There's a scene in the first movie where a little boy is talking to Neo, one of the central characters. The young boy sits in front of six spoons, all twisted and contorted. He is holding yet another spoon, gazing at it intently as the spoon softens, melts, then bends in half. He appears to be bending the spoons with his mind. The central character, Neo, looks on, stunned and in disbelief about how he can do what he's doing.

The little boy looks up at Neo, hands him the spoon, and says, "Don't try to bend the spoon. That's impossible. Instead, only try to realize the truth." Neo says, "What truth?" The boy replies, "There is no spoon. There is only ourselves." Neo looks at him, then back at the spoon. He focuses all his attention on it. After a few seconds, he, too, bends the spoon.

I love that. This example shows that you don't have to practice a great deal to shift your mindset. You just have to grasp the truth, and you can change your vibration immediately. To me, the spoon represents an object, situation, or circumstance in our lives. Most of the time, we are focused on changing those situations. In other words, "bending the spoon," right?

Maybe your spoon is your boss or your husband. It might be your child, a roommate, or your significant other. It could be your financial situation, school, career path, or parents. It doesn't matter. When we're focused on the situation, the object (spoon) itself, we're giving a lot of power to that particular thing. The real energy, the real power –the real way that things shift – is when you put that energy and the focus back on you.

Try it yourself. Take a spoon, pen, or pencil and hold it loosely between your thumb and forefinger. Now wave your hand up and down quickly so the object moves. Watch it. If you do it right, it will "appear to bend." It's just an illusion, but it looks real. When a professional does it, it appears even more flexible. Even though you know it's an illusion, it seems real to you.

We may think that if we just concentrate hard – really, really hard – on bending that spoon, then we can bend it, too. We can't. That's the point. When you're putting all of the emphasis and the ability on the object, you lose sight of the fact that you're the one that has the ability to bend life around you. You can do this using the powers within you. When you realize it's your mindset that needs to shift and not the spoon, then it will be easy. When you understand that you've got the power to do anything and can see the spoon as bent, then it's already done. It's simple.

### ARE PEOPLE REALLY SEEING YOU?

We all know how good it feels to be seen for who we really are. But often, we don't validate this feeling as being important in our lives. The people around you, particularly if they're your children or your boss, aren't necessarily going to tell you all the time that they see you and appreciate you. This doesn't mean they don't think it, or even that they don't want to hear it said about them.

Indeed, absolutely everybody wants to be seen for who they really are. Everybody wants to be valued and appreciated. That value and appreciation is not about receiving praise for how you cook the greatest eggs, or how you make a serious impact to the bottom line. It's about seeking the true value and appreciation for who we are at our core. As the song

"Who Will Love Me For Me" by JJ Heller[8] goes:

*"Could you send someone here who will love me?*
*Who will love me for me*
*Not for what I have done or what I will become*
*Who will love me for me*
*Cause nobody has shown me what love really means."*

Regardless of the ways people might present themselves, everyone thinks about and wants that kind of love. We all want it. It's a part of being human. Sometimes the more we want and need it, the better we hide our desire for it from others.

I can think of a couple of fairly recent scenarios. I am an owner of a business, and I have some great partnerships in my business. In one of my partnerships, we make a good amount of money, and we make a difference in our clients' businesses. I am very proud of these accomplishments and the relationships I've developed in the process.

Sometimes, however, people will acknowledge the work that I'm bringing to the table, but rarely see me for who I believe I truly am. This manifests most frequently in their lack of acknowledgment of my empathetic nature. They don't see the empathy that I show in our relationship, or in the relationships that we have with our clients. This empathy allows me to provide a service that might not be obvious in a tangible way. The empathy that I'm bringing to the table has allowed some of our solutions to be quite stellar. It's not something that is tangibly black and white, or something I can point to on a slide or in a bulleted memo.

Some of the people with whom I work do many things in the community that are very high profile. They believe being high profile is the best way to enact positive social change. They have told me as much when they have stated things, "You don't really know what it's like to make a difference because you're on the outskirts of life."

Statements like the above are hard for me to hear when I know, besides the formal mentoring programs and other community activities

---

8   https://www.youtube.com/watch?v=uWKkdgyJ_NI

in which I take part, I am constantly helping others. I use my intuition, knowing when people are in need, listening for their stated and unstated needs, coaching them through their lives. I love helping others in so many ways, day-to-day. However, to be told I'm not making a big difference hurt a great deal.

When I think about these types of relationship and comments like that, it doesn't feel good at all. Yet I keep doing what I'm doing because I'm not doing it for that person and their validation. I'm doing it because it fulfills me, and I develop strong relationships with many other amazing people in the process.

Conversely, I have a good friend, Mike, with whom I sometimes do business. However, I consider him to be a life coach for me. He will just stop and make it a point to literally say the words, "*I see you.* You're making such a big difference in the lives of people, and I already know that it has a ripple effect. It's not just what you're doing with this person and that person. I know that based on who you're being, it has a ripple effect in the world and the people around you. Thank you for being that way. Thank you for being vulnerable day-to-day. Thank you for your intuition."

This friend encourages me all the time to make decisions based on that intuition because he sees me. He really sees me. He knows the accuracy of who I am as opposed to others who might say that it's not fact-based enough, so we shouldn't go in that direction.

Terry Tilman writes about an experience he had in Africa twenty years ago when he was on safari. He said as he traveled through the villages and Serengeti savanna, he noticed that when one of the indigenous people would approach another, they would pause, face each other, look directly in each other's' eyes for 5-15 seconds, say something, and then continue on their way. This would happen in populated villages and in very remote areas. When he finally asked his guide about this practice, he was told the people were greeting each other. "How are they doing that? What are they saying?" Tilman asked.

The guide said, "One of them says, 'I see you.' Connecting through the eyes, the other replies, 'I am here.'"

This, some say, was probably where writers for the movie *Avatar* got the most powerful phrase used in the movie, "I see you," something that the natives used to greet each other.

The other thing Tilman's guide told him was that in the native's language, the greeting also meant something like "Until you see me, I do not exist. When you see me, you bring me into existence."[9]

I can promise you there's a really big difference between my friend Mike, who sees me very clearly, and my other friend, who does not. While Mike is certainly supportive of the business that I do, most of his words of value and appreciation have to do with who I really am. His seeing that part of me and appreciating and promoting it make it so much easier for me to continue doing what I do. "I see you." It's what parents say to their children at soccer games, in the swimming pool, or anytime their child wants their attention or support. "I see you." So simple, but so powerful. Try it.

As I think about the power of seeing others, I started thinking about a pattern that sometimes occurs when there's a challenge in my family. I'm an only child, so we're all pretty close. If something is going on with one of us, it's going on for all three of us.

The other day, there was an issue with my mom's car, and my dad thought she should get a new car. My mom didn't want to get a new car. My dad left the house, and my mother and I were talking. We were dreading him coming back home and the big disagreement we were all going to have about this car situation. As I was visiting, I couldn't really escape this situation. I thought I'd have to bear down and just go through it with them. That's typically how it goes in my family.

At first, I was focused on my father, focused on hoping that he would take a different position, focused on the hope and even the prayer that he would hear my mother's side, and focused on hoping that she would hear his side. Then it hit me to use what I know. I decided that it wasn't about focusing on either one of them.

Instead of focusing on them and trying to change their perspectives, I started to focus on the experience that I wanted to have. I was there to have a nice visit, and that's what I decided to focus on, no matter what.

---

9  http://www.finerminds.com/consciousness-awareness/samburu-greeting-terry-tillman/

I stopped even entertaining what they might or might not do or say. I chose to focus on feeling peaceful and staying in a peaceful, calm state of mind regardless of what they or anybody else did. I quit thinking about it and began to already know that I had the power to feel good and peaceful, period. I lay down with my dog and watched some television, and when dad came in, it was a completely uneventful evening.

When they did end up talking about it, he had actually completely changed his perspective. Now, some might say he had time to think about it or find some other reason for his behavior, but what I know is I withdrew my energy and focus from the potential negative consequences. Therefore, I wasn't a part of creating whatever that dynamic was. Because I happened to be sitting with my mother, she fed off of my energy, which was really calm and not focused on the car situation anymore, so she was in that place as well. We had the power within us to stay in a peaceful place, a calm place. When you know that, when you understand that power that you have, it not only impacts your life but can impact those around you.

Seeing yourself for who you really are begins with being present to *your life, your situation,* and *your intuition.* This is Step 1. If I happened to be the First Lady of the United States or the Queen of England and you were my daughter or son, no matter what you're going through, the response would still be the same. In spite of who you are, where you come from, the money, position, power, or status you may have, negative things still happen, no matter what your lot in life is. You'll still experience death, disease, and all sorts of things. People break up with you. It doesn't mean that you're absent from life.

But if you think about some of the things that you are challenged with right now, imagine you're someone you're not. What if I said that you were the First Lady of the United States, Queen of England, or King of Zimbabwe? I believe that you would respond differently to the challenge or the dreams you have. There would be a sense that "I come from royalty. I've got all this power here. I have resources. I have money. I have people who want to support me." You can see that very easily because it's tangible, and we all know what comes with those types of positions and powers in life.

It's the same thing with being a woman. You really do come from absolute greatness. You are the being that was born to birth things, to create things, to bring another human life into the world. You have an intuition that's unparalleled. You have empathy and an ability to listen that's unparalleled.

Step 1 is to remember who you are. This step is about realizing that you were born with a certain level of power. When you're thinking about focusing on the spoon and you say, "I wish the spoon would bend," the real thought is "I'm so powerful. Of course, it's going to bend. I am a part of everything. We're all connected. This is easy. I create my reality." That's a lot different from thinking, "I've got to focus on the spoon, and I hope it bends. I wish it would. I don't even know if it can. Maybe only these kinds of people can do it or a magician can do it." You were born to be powerful.

Step 2 is to focus on what it is that you want and move in that direction. To go back to our example of *The Matrix*, for those of you who are not familiar with the film, there is a central character who is considered to be the chosen one who can do so many incredible things. But he doubted himself. He wasn't really sure who he was, even when everyone else was. Quite frankly, it seemed unbelievable that he could be this special. But the moment in the movie when he recognized that he really was the chosen one – as we all are – moving forward was a no-brainer. Suddenly he knew exactly what to do, how to act, what his purpose was.

It's the same with you. Once you understand who you are and what you are meant to be, you begin to do just what you would naturally do if you'd known all along. Trying to figure out what to do next isn't an issue. You don't even worry about it because you know you'll be inspired to the very next thought as you need it.

Now, that doesn't mean you're invincible. Superhero or not, you're still human with very real human needs, which brings us to the concept of self-care.

## SELF-CARE

Self-care is one of the most important ideas in this book. It's a topic many of us hear about on daytime talk shows. We talk about it in spas and book clubs and even at work, but it's still not something that we seem to incorporate day-to-day. For most of us, when we think of self-care, we think of it like this: "I'm going to schedule time to get a massage, get my hair done, or just be alone for an hour sometime next month." Or "I'm going to take a vacation." We think that caring for our exterior is what self-care is all about – smooth skin, firm muscles, relaxed body parts.

All of those are certainly elements of self-care, and I strongly and highly recommend that you do them. I'm a huge spa fan and look forward to having many more spa-related retreats in my life. But self-care is something that happens every day, all day, beyond the walls of the spa. Self-care is about loving yourself first and loving yourself enough to put yourself first.

For so many women, we have a bizarre definition of obligation that prevents us from allowing ourselves the self-care that we need. On a high level, we all know that many of us are both mothers and working outside of the home. Perhaps we don't have children, but maybe we're working in the community and are involved in multiple initiatives that pull us in different directions. This is nothing new.

What I'm not sure of is whether we are willing to get really honest about some of the subtle obligations that prevent us from taking care of ourselves.

As an example, I have some great friends in my life. I can think about one in particular, I'll call her Sheri, with whom I occasionally do business. I am sometimes more detailed about things than Sheri. There have been a number of occasions when we have come together, each having done a particular part of a project. Yet Sheri didn't have her portion of the project completed because some other things were going on in her life. Because I consider Sheri a friend and because we were doing business together, I decided to continue to move forward and just do what I needed to do to get the project done.

But, when I really started to take a look at how I was letting Sheri take advantage of me, I realized my feelings of obligation to make sure the project didn't suffer, were preventing me from taking care of myself. I was taking on more work than I needed to.

When I had time to further examine my thoughts, I remembered that I'm responsible only for myself. And Sheri was responsible for herself.

Secret #4: It's Not The Spoon That Bends; It's You

This didn't mean that sometimes I wouldn't go the extra mile for others like Sheri. But it did mean that I needed to begin to recognize – day by day, moment by moment – those times when I might feel a subtle obligation to take on more than I should and that this feeling of obligation would prevent me from providing the best self-care for me.

My self talk in this situation with Sheri went something like, "Well, if I don't step up, will I still be seen as a good friend? If I don't do this, will this project fail? If I don't do this, will I seem inflexible? If I don't do this, will I be as rigid as some of the other people that I've complain about in other parts of my work life? Am I not showing up like a woman by creating my own boundaries in this relationship?"

All of my worries were built on obligation, not love though. I realized that I wasn't taking care of myself. I needed to protect my own time. If we are supposed to have dinner and I show up on time and haven't eaten since lunch because I was waiting on dinner—and now the dinner is an hour late—that's not self-care because now I've got a headache and my stomach hurts.

When you compromise your boundaries, you will fail to get what you need. What you need can be very different from what others need. You may need a certain amount of alone time to function at your best. Ask yourself, "Do I get reenergized by being around people, or do I get energized by just having some time alone?" Do you get that need met or not?

I know I need to eat regularly or I'm not so pleasant.

Are you on a schedule where you are not allowing yourself to just eat? Many of us are. We go hours and hours without eating because we feel obligated to do these other things. Self-care would be making sure that you're on an eating schedule and you're mindful of the fact that you haven't eaten and that you're sacrificing your body and mind for someone else. Again, we all do it, but are we doing it consistently? What's getting in the way?

What else do you need to feel good? Is it great conversation and wine? Is it great sex with your partner? Is it taking a walk? Whatever those things are, are we waiting for the vacation to do it or the weekend or some other future time? Or, are we being mindful of these small things that we can do daily to take care of ourselves?

We're really unstoppable when we're in full alignment with ourselves.

When we're not taking care of ourselves, we just can't be our best. Have we all learned to do it? Sure. Here's the catch. Most of us are high functioning. Our not-so-great is still great! But imagine how productive you would be if you were actually eating in a nutritious way. Imagine if you were moving in the way that you should. Just moving your body. I'm not saying you've got to work out for 30 minutes a day, but I'm saying movement, versus just sitting at a desk or in a daycare or whatever it is that you do day-to-day, matters. Imagine how much better it would be if your mind, body, and spirit were all in alignment.

Sometimes, when talking about self-care, women can feel like it's something that they've mastered, that they don't need it unless it's a big vacation or a big spa day or something like that. There are some powerful women who have gotten so used to not taking care of themselves, it's almost a conversation that is beneath them. There's a belief that this is just a part of the price of success. I want to say very clearly that it's simply not true.

I can tell you from experience because I had a stroke, and I believe it was the cumulative effect of a lack of self-care. I was going through a divorce and, grateful to say, with very little disagreement. Quite frankly, it should have been finished quickly as I did not ask for a dime of what I was entitled to in our short marriage. However, even though we agreed on the terms in writing, he did not sign the paperwork for approximately eleven months. I'm sure he had his reasons, none of which were disclosed to me.

During that time period, I felt mentally stuck because I didn't have the signed paper to say the marriage was over. I kept my concerns bottled inside. I didn't feel I had the right to complain since we were not in huge fights like so many of my friends had experienced. However, I was under significant financial strain, and emotionally, I felt like I couldn't move. During this time, I did not practice self-care. I wasn't there for my own emotional health, and I worked tirelessly to get my business off the ground. One day after experiencing severe chest, arm, and back pain, I drove myself to the ER. Even that was telling, making the choice to drive myself versus allowing medical professionals to assist me by calling an ambulance or asking family or friends for help. Recovery was quick, about 3 months. I credit that to my understanding of how to deliberately create.

Our male counterparts, while they are working just as hard and experiencing life changing events too, often have other people in their lives who take care of some of the things for them that you take care of on your own. There's an amount of self-care that they're allowed to give to themselves that we're not always afforded because we're doing our work and we're doing some extra.

If you're in a business environment, you rarely find men saying, "Gosh, I'm really tired," but you hear women saying it all the time. "I'm so busy, I'm so busy, I'm so busy." Somehow, men find a way to take the time that they need. If it's in the middle of the day for golf, or if it's when they get home and declare that they need some time, that's what happens.

But when we get home, we just move on to the next thing that we've got to do. My goal here is to provide tangible ways to help you take better care of yourself.

## BEING SHREWD

Shrewd is a term synonymous with men or high-powered business women. While this may be true, the need to be astute or sharp in practical matters should apply to us all. We should be shrewd in our focus, be shrewd in our actions and in our commitment to ourselves, every day.

When there's something that you're really wanting to experience, be shrewd about having it at all costs. When I say "at all costs," I don't mean to act in a way that's not integrous. I mean you should not be distracted by things that are going on around you. Be shrewd and focused to the point that even if the people closest to you don't think you can do it, or it doesn't make any sense, or you don't have enough money in the bank for it right now, none of that will deter you from continuing to move in a particular direction.

It's not because you're focused on the spoon. It's about recognizing the power you have within you, opening up those super powers in your vault and allowing them to shine through. There's a shrewdness to that. This means you have to say "no" to some things to stay focused on you. You become shrewd when you realize that "I'm this powerful and really nothing can get in my way."

## COURAGE

Courage: is it nature or nurture? There are people who I know that have been courageous since we were children. It felt like nothing ever scared them. No matter what it was, they were never afraid. Even if there was a risk, they could acknowledge it, but they moved forward with an incredible amount of confidence. Then there are others, like me – depending on what the situation is – for whom fear is very real. I've got to do some work to get there. I've got to decide if I'm willing to risk it, to fight the fear.

An interesting thing about courage is that it's a choice. Sometimes, when you're seeing people do great things, it almost feels like they've got something special going on. But it's really a choice. I think about the times that I've chosen to be courageous. When it was over, I recognized that the fear was ultimately unfounded. It doesn't mean that I didn't have to go through some steps. But oftentimes, they were nowhere close to what I anticipated. A lot of times, fear is based on a grandiose, unrealistic vision of what we think is going to happen. But you can only live in this particular moment. There's nothing you can do at any other time but right now.

Courage is usually about choice. Think about the times when you had courage and you walked through a particular challenge. Consider these things: Was it as bad as you thought? As you moved through whatever it was that you were worried about, did you make it? Are you still here? Of course. If not, you wouldn't be reading this book.

It's about taking steps to be courageous. Once you recognize this power that's within, you'll be guided to the next step. People will show up in your life to help you through difficult times. It's about deciding to be courageous more than anything else.

### LEARN HOW TO FOCUS

When I was in my freshman year of college, my father came with me and registered me for all of my classes, even choosing when I would start and end each of my days! It took me an entire year after that to realize I could register on my own. And that's just what I did in my sophomore year. I finally realized ... I was free! I could make my own choices! I could come and go as I pleased! My parents were in another state, and I was FREE!

So I set my own schedule. Instead of starting in the very early hours of the morning (I am by no means a morning person), I started my classes at 10:00. Then I found out that by starting that late, I had to schedule my classes until 7:00 p.m. At first, that was fine. I was doing what I had chosen. But then I began to realize that I was stuck at school later and later while my friends were out having fun. Also, when I was in night class, I would find myself too tired to do my homework for my next day of class. Meanwhile, my friends had focused their efforts on getting their work done before the evening so they could have some fun at night. I started cutting classes here and there. Eventually, it became a habit that spiraled out of control. I haphazardly decided that many of my classes were not worth attending.

The semester zoomed by. I was having such a good time that I didn't even notice it was coming to an abrupt end. Suddenly, classes ended and grades were out. I hesitated to look online at my grades, but I reluctantly did so anyway. Ouch! They were terrible!

In addition to being very authoritative, my father was (and still is) an educator. Academic probation was absolutely unacceptable to him.

I panicked. What was I going to do? I called a woman I knew who had mentored me using a lot of the strategies and tactics I describe in this book. I told her that I'd gotten these poor grades and that they would signify to my father that I was on probation. I told her that in the school I was attending being on probation would mean I would have to sit out a semester.

She responded to my panicky comment, "Erika, I want you to focus exclusively on what you want until something changes in this regard ... for the better. Don't call me until *something changes*."

Later that day, I went to work at the site for my semester internship, a hotel. Anytime that I wasn't actively involved with a hotel guest, I was thinking only about coming back to school the next semester and doing well. That's all I thought about ... period.

At that end of that first day of implementing this strategy, I decided to call the dean of my school to say, "These are my grades. What are my options?" I called her, taking one deep breath after another. I did have a lofty hope that things would turn out okay, but I was still as nervous as heck.

The dean took my call with a cheery voice. I remember thinking her voice would perhaps not sound as cheery once she saw my grades. Then, something strange happened. After the unbearably long pause in time for her to look up my grades, she came back on the phone and stated with a lilt in her voice, "I see that your grades are low, but for some reason, the computer did not place you on probation. You are the luckiest girl that I know. I've never seen this happen before. Why are you not on probation?"

I could only whisper back, "I don't know."

She then added, "If the computer is not going to put you on probation, I'm not going to manually do it either. You should take this as a sign to get yourself together and do what you need to do next semester to end this losing streak."

That's just what I did.

### STAY FOCUSED DESPITE WHAT YOU'RE SEEING

Let's say you're challenged in your workplace in some way. You've got people coming in your office constantly asking you for help with something that they're doing. You've not set any policies or procedures in place in your office about disruptions, so you're getting interrupted constantly. You may also have interruptions from an ailing parent or your significant other who is in need of something because he/she is in career transition.

You could have any number of outside influences that are dissipating your focus. With that, you ask the question, "How do I make this happen when I feel like I'm bombarded daily?" This is not uncommon. According to the *Washington Post*, we can have up to six hours of distractions coming at us each day.

### PRESCRIPTION FOR DEALING WITH DISTRACTIONS.

My prescription is partly adapted from one of my favorite coaches, Tony Robbins. Start every morning with three and a half minutes of gratitude.

To be more specific, you might take one to three things that you are specifically grateful for and focus on those.

For me, when I wake up and my dog is at the foot of my bed and I see her there, there's such an amazing love that I feel for the dog. And I know she loves me back. This helps me immerse myself in gratitude for the love that we share. I can also feel that same level of gratitude for the people who are supporting me in writing this book. It's just an overwhelming feeling of gratitude.

You live in this gratitude. You live there for three to five minutes. This is important because two diametrically opposed thoughts, feelings, and/or emotions cannot occupy the same space. If you're in a place of gratitude, you won't be in a scattered place, a place of worry, of fear, or distraction. You're just right there in the feeling of gratitude.

Next, think about the two or three positive outcomes that you're focused on. I don't mean for today, but for the future. Where are you going in the next six months? In the next year? Who are you becoming? State those positive outcomes as if they are already there. For example, "I am an international bestseller." Focus there, and you will anchor those outcomes, those things that you desire, from a state of gratefulness, not from a state of distraction, worry, or fear. This will create an elevated, high vibrational state from which all positive things are created. Hold that vibration as long as possible.

#### FOCUS OR LUCK?

Since that day, I have continued to practice the power of focus. I *know* how powerful it is. I know that if I focus exclusively on what I choose, I have a much better chance of getting it than if I just HOPE something will happen. I *know* I'm also more powerful when someone else joins me in focusing on a particular thing or situation. With two or more people, together and focused, we create an even more powerful attractor for what we have chosen. Either alone or in a group, when we select and focus, we are able to manifest what we desire. Following are three steps you can use to get focused quickly:

**First, focus on what you want—but use the word 'choose' as it will**

**move you from lacking to empowered.** But it's okay if you start with the word 'want' and then shift as you get more acclimated around the process.

**Second, decide the steps you can take to get what you choose.** Every goal contains steps to reach it. Start with your goal and then work backwards from the vision of what reaching that goal looks like, sounds like, feels like, etc.

**Third, plan how you will stay focused when distractions swarm around you.** Here, being *proactive* will keep you developing what you choose, bringing it to your doorstep earlier rather than later. Think of any of the hurdles you might face and, one by one, figure out how you will address each hurdle *if* it appears. I don't mean the tactical things you are going to do. I mean, who are you going to be? How will you think and feel? This way you will indeed stay focused, no matter what.

Few people realize that focus is an integral part of creating anything that you choose. You've actually been hearing it all your life. Remember when you were in school? Your teachers told you to focus on what they were saying or to focus on doing your homework. If you were ever in any sports, your coach told you to focus. Or perhaps you were musically inclined, and your piano or other music teacher told you to focus.

We know we should be focusing, but we don't understand how powerful focus really is. We also don't know how to do it. The first thing to do to focus effectively is to remain calm. Think about people who are wildly successful. Whether you like them or not, whether you care for their personalities or not, the one thing you'll notice about them is that they are focused—at all costs—on what it is that they want.

Think about someone like Donald Trump who has amassed a lot of money, lost it, and gained it again. You may or may not like him, but the one thing that you know about him is he's focused on winning. He will tell you that. At all times, no matter what, his intention is to win. You've got to have that same sort of almost blind focus to get what you want.

Now that we know the power of focus, part of the challenge is not knowing what to focus on. Sometimes we're simply not clear on what we want. As I mentioned earlier, you've got to know what you want in order to focus. The way that your brain works is that it does what you ask it to do. If you are focused on things that you are unclear about or that change from one moment to the next, you will get inconsistent results or no results at all.

### STEP ONE: GET CLEAR ON WHAT YOU WANT – VIBRATIONS

We are all vibrations. You're always attracting, vibrationally, that which you really are and that which you're focused on. If you are not clear, the universe – the powers and energy within the universe – cannot manifest something that you've not outlined clearly for yourself. So Step One is always to get clear on what you want.

The key to doing this is to not care what other people think. Easier said than done, right? For example, you might think, "People are going to be mad at me or they will tell me I'm a dreamer or laugh at me when I tell them my dreams."

Whatever you imagine or whatever their remarks are regarding your path, make it no concern of yours. It is coming *through* their heads into their mouths. These are not your thoughts but theirs. When you experience their opinions, smile, and just say "thanks!" In your own mind, give back to them the thoughts they gave to you. You might also try saying something like "I know those are your opinions. Thank you. I know if you had similar dreams I would be right there supporting you."

Then come right back to your focus. You have already told yourself your intentions. You are taking action around your intentions and, sooner rather than later, with focus, you will start building up a network of people who mirror back to you the same positive thoughts you intend for yourself and even for them. Now you will have *mutually beneficial* exchanges with them. This is what my colleague, Melissa G. Wilson, bestselling author of the book *Networlding,* and her co-author, first Chief Marketing Officer of Motorola Jocelyn Carter Miller, discovered after two decades of research.

This involves choosing strategic exchanges with *like-valued* people who are all about giving to others rather than constantly taking. For example, say one of your top values is being a person with integrity. When you find others who hold integrity as a top value, your conversations with them will be highly effective and fruitful. You are now on the same page! You two are focused and dynamically exchanging ideas, connections, and great opportunities with each other. Doesn't that sound like the way to reach your goals?

## WHAT DO YOU NEED?

The next step in the focusing process is to ask yourself, "What am I in need of right now?" Are you in need of support to keep your focus going? Are you in need of a *shift* in the people who are currently in your life? Are you in need of other particular resources that will help you stay focused? Many of us think about what we need in terms of what others *need from us,* as in, "I need to be a better daughter, wife, spouse, mother, boss, or employee." Imagine there is no one else. You're on a deserted island and have only yourself to worry about. Now ... what do *you* need?

Many times your needs reflect the collective of the five people that you're around most often. Discover what it is that you're in need of so that you can make requests that will support you. *Choose* to find that support for yourself. This could look like seeking help from an outside source such as a coach, mentor, or peer whom you admire. It could mean searching for books or information in articles and blogs that provide insight. It could involve taking that course that would be the next step in your path to reach your goal. This step doesn't have to be hard when your mind and heart are in alignment. So what's next?

After focus and choosing what you want and need, the next step involves playing to win. This is about seeing your goal line where you have not only accomplished your dream but you are appreciative that you have arrived where you intended to be—at the finish line, as the winner.

Many of us get sidetracked because we don't always play to win. Often, this is because we have formed relationships with others who don't have similar or complementary values to ours. You may get scared or feel like you should compromise because others are not supporting your goals. Here, in this latter situation, others may superimpose their fears or jealousies on you. You stop playing to win. Yet, if you stay the course and play to win, the universe will support you. This is a certainty.

In one of my favorite books, *Nice Girls Don't Get the Corner Office,* the author shares a chapter showcasing one of the biggest mistakes women make in their lives. It's called *fait accompli*. This is a French term that means certain things that occur in our lives are irreversible or predetermined. However, *nothing* is irreversible or predetermined when you: 1) know your choices, and 2) stay focused on what you choose, not taking your eyes off your goal.

## ASK YOURSELF "WHO AM I TODAY?

Every single day, you have a choice. You have the option to create and be who you want to be. You don't have to focus on yesterday or any other day in the past. State out loud, "Today, I am an amazing leader. Today, I am a fantastic daughter. Today, I am a wonderful mother. Today, I'm going to show love in this way. Today, I'm going to communicate through my true, authentic voice." This part of the process is called "setting your intentions." Your goal is to *declare your intentions for each and every day.*

These declarations set your foundation for each day. They also anchor you to what you said in the morning. As things are moving and swirling around you, the positive and powerful anchor you set for yourself that morning gives you the ability to go back to where you started the day. Note that in the middle of the day, when people are coming at you with all sorts of things, it's okay to take three minutes and go back to gratitude. The point is you've got to keep yourself in a positive vibration as much as you can throughout the day so that you can draw more of your positive intentions to you.

It will help to discover things that you can refer to that keep you anchored to what you talked about in the morning. There might be a song that is in alignment with where you're going. It could be a picture of your children or something you're striving for – a home, a car, or new relationships. Keep those pictures that you use to support where you're going present in your mind. It will be much easier to maintain a positive connection to your declarations. This is where vision boards can be helpful.

Throughout the day, we get distracted by things that are constantly happening in the outside world. It's extremely difficult to completely avoid distraction. Understanding this is key. If, however, you have something to refer to quickly, like a picture, song, or strong sense memory of how you felt earlier in the day or before bed, it's easier to get yourself back on track.

In his book *Feel it Real,* Neville Goddard used a neuroscience perspective to explain that when there's something that you desire, not only should you stay focused on it, but you've got to actually *feel it* as if it's real. Feeling the vibration, experiencing that feeling, is a step beyond visualization. Many times, with visualization, you're looking at the event from the outside.

As an example, if you choose a new car, you start visualizing it. But "feeling it real" involves getting even closer to the experience of having your car, actually being inside of it, feeling all the nuances of your first time in your new car—from the uber-comfortable leather seats to the beautiful dashboard, skylights, and, of course, that unmistakable new car smell! Really see your new car. You would see the hood of your car, the steering wheel, upgraded radio and stereo system. You would see your right hand with that ring that you wear every day as it hits against the wood part of the steering wheel. You would see your left hand resting on the side part of the window.

When you are inside of the car, you can't help but feel what it's like to be in that place. This is the way to keep your focus going by feeling it real, feeling how smooth the car is driving as you accelerate, how comfortable it is to be in your new car versus one that perhaps has had some problems in the past. You can feel the admiring eyes on you as you cruise down the street.

### FEELINGS AND FOCUS

Feeling it real helps to cement your goal or vision into your physiology, which always helps to manifest what your thoughts are and then bring your visions into reality. They will manifest in your positive and consistent vibration. Move from just thinking about your intentions to feeling them real. This allows you to anchor your new choices. Even if you think about the things that are most memorable to you, you don't just hold the *thought* of those things, but even more so, the *feelings* you once had that created them. Feelings are what stay with you, whether what you received was something great or something painful. These feelings create your anchors.

I'm going to give you an example of using the power of "feeling it real" to effect significant change. James Nesbeth was your average amateur golfer, a military man who loved the game but confined most of his practice to weekend games with buddies and the occasional long drive session. He routinely shot in the mid- to low-90s. Though he tried to improve, he rarely saw much of a difference despite physical practice.

As active military personnel, Major Nesbeth was assigned to overseas duty fairly regularly. On one such tour, he was captured in North Vietnam and held in a small cell as a prisoner of war. His cage was approximately four and a half feet high and five feet long. He was held in this cage for seven years.

During the first few months of his imprisonment, Nesbeth almost exclusively hoped and prayed for his release. He saw no one, he talked to no one, and he had no physical activity. He quickly realized that hoping and praying would get him nowhere. He had to cement a vision in his mind of something he wanted to accomplish or he would go insane with the lack of stimulation. So he decided to focus on one thing he loved that he knew he could imagine and make real to him in his confinement: golf.

Every day for seven straight years, Nesbeth visualized playing golf. Each day he would select a golf course and play through all 18 holes in their entirety. He experienced every sensation, sight, smell, sound, and taste to the fullest extent possible. He felt the grass crunch under his feet. He saw the sun blazing on the bright sand of the sand traps. He felt each club in his hands, the putters lighter, the drivers heavier as he swung. And he imagined what it would feel like to swing the club and score under par in a huge variety of different scenarios.

He would instruct himself as he swung, reminding himself to keep his head up and his eyes on the ball. Then he watched the ball arc through the air, bounce, and land exactly where he imagined his swing would take it. It took him just as long to play each imaginary 18 holes as it did in real life – four hours. Thus, for four hours a day, seven days a week, fifty-two weeks a year, for seven years, Major James Nesbeth visualized playing golf down to every last detail.

When he was released, Nesbeth came home and went to his beloved golf course to play a round with his buddies. On his first game back, Nesbeth shot a 74. He had taken twenty strokes off his game simply by visualizing a better outcome. Nesbeth had mastered "feeling it real," and it manifested in a virtually unheard of improvement in his game despite the physical toll that imprisonment had taken on his body.[10]

While this example is extreme, Nesbeth's methods illustrate the very strong power that feeling your intentions real can have on your life. What feelings can you use to anchor your intentions? In what ways do you *feel* that help you positively choose to act? How will you "feel it real" in your day-to-day life?

## Action Steps

1. Focus on what you want at all costs.
2. Shift from *wanting it* to *choosing it.*
3. *Play to Win.* This is about seeing your goal line where you have accomplished your dream and are in that state of great appreciation that you arrived where you intended to be—at the finish line, as the winner.
4. From your heart, figure out what you need.
5. Stay focused in the midst of what you're seeing by using support strategies such as a coach, books, articles, a buddy, etc.
6. Feel your choices as real.
7. Go through these steps before you go to bed and when you wake up.

---

10  Adapted from http://www.inspirationalstories.com/5/537.html, but I think the original version is in *A 2nd Helping of Chicken Soup for the Soul.*

# CHAPTER 7

# Secret #5: Success Comes From Leading With Feminine Power

In 2014, Janet Yellen, then 67 years old, became the first woman to run the United States Federal Reserve Board. She earned this position after working with the Federal Reserve for over thirty years.

Sheryl Sandberg, like Mark Zuckerberg, attended Harvard. Unlike Zuckerberg, who dropped out of college his sophomore year to pursue a new project we all now know as Facebook, Sandberg finished her degree, graduating at the top of the economics department. Her first job out of school was at Google where she became a business unit general manager in 2001, then later the VP for Global Online Sales and Operations. After seven years with Google, she started looking for another job and ended up at Facebook, now a multi-billion dollar operation where she became the COO (Chief Operations Officer) and a billionaire herself.

Mary Barra is a wife, mother, and her family's designated grocery shopper by night, but by day she is the CEO of General Motors. She manages to combine family and a career.

There are others, millions of women who run their own businesses, act as CEOs, COOs, directors, and board members of the organizations and businesses that shape the world we live in. But while there are millions of women with tremendous presence and impact around the world, the majority of the force that's shaping the world is still predominantly made up of men. According to the latest survey by Catalyst, a nonprofit that tracks gender parity in the workplace, women occupy a measly 4% of the corner offices at S&P 500 companies and hold only 25% of executive or senior-level jobs in those same firms. The good news is that since 2005, the number of women who are world leaders—presidents or heads of state—has more than doubled, according to the Pew Research Center.[11]

I hope that changes soon occur in the gender statistics of executive positions that parallel the recent boost of females as world leaders. Now, besides being women, what do these leaders have in common? They all lead with feminine power. People used to believe (and many still do) that the only way for a woman to succeed in fields where men typically dominate, including business, the military, or tech, was to act, dress, and lead like a man. The pundits were wrong. There's another kind of power in the world. It's the power of creativity, conception, nurture, and emotions. It's feminine power.

The concept of feminine power is still misunderstood, even by women themselves. It has nothing to do with gender and everything to do with the vibration of the feminine. Feminine power is:

- Cultivating your authentic self – that inner quality that self-affirms your life, identify, well-being, and purpose, whether it's raising children, directing a board meeting, or being a CEO.

- The confidence to recognize that if you lose a job, relationship, or opportunity, something bigger and better will come along.

- Having an emotional backbone. Women with emotional backbones hold their men, bosses, employees, friends, and business partners to higher standards. They operate with fearlessness, and they don't seek the attention and approval of others. They are

---

11  https://www.forbes.com/sites/alixmcnamara/2016/06/06/the-worlds-most-powerful-women-in-2016/#569862d71c83

self-contained. They prefer being respected to being liked.

- Being self-actualized. It's not that women with feminine power somehow bypassed challenges, failures, fears, and disempowerment. Rather, they encountered everything life and failure could throw at them, rose above it, and learned from it.

The concept of leading with feminine power explains our power to conceive and create rather than control and destroy. Really, there is nothing else, other than a higher power/God, that can give birth to life and ideas the way that women can. As women, we can give birth and create another living being.

Women have created cultures and subcultures that go beyond developing technology or methods of efficiently running homes. We are a critical force in forming attitudes and ethical concerns and standards. We are in the captain's chair when it comes to determining where society will move. According to the National Women's Business Council, women currently own 8 million businesses with an economic impact of $3 trillion. This statistically translates into the creation and/or maintenance of 23 million jobs, or 16% of all U.S. jobs.[12]

And our influence is growing. According to SBA's Office of Advocacy:

*... 99.7 percent of all employer firms are classified as "small businesses (less than 500 employees);" small businesses employ 51% of all people; have generated nearly two-thirds (64%) of net new jobs over the past decade and a half; and produce 13 times more patents per employee than large patenting firms. From 1997-2002, women-owned firms were growing at twice the rate of all other groups and while the current economic woes have dampened business growth for all segments, women continue to keep pace. However, in most public conversations and in most people's minds, the important player in the economy is the large corporations – which only account for .03 percent of all firms and employ fewer people than small businesses do in total. This*

---

12 https://www.nwbc.gov/research/economic-impact-women-owned-business-
es-united-states

*research illuminates the economic reality and calls for changing the conversation at a policy level and in the public sphere.*

*What would happen if women-owned firms were not in the economy and generating this $2.8 trillion in economic impact? An additional 16 percent of our labor force would be jobless – that's 23 million people!"* [13]

Think about ancient civilizations where people came together to exchange ideas and develop new ways of doing things. We weren't just creating a space where we could survive. We were creating society and culture, and setting the tone for the future. We were not only taking care of children, but also all women, grandmothers, and mothers. As women, we were nurturing everyone, not just the children. We were developing an environment that existed for and impacted everyone. From rituals of birth to transition from puberty to adulthood, women set the tone regarding their importance. We handed down our healing, intuition, dances, songs, clothing designs, and stories to generations of tribal members, and all were created by or influenced by women.

As creators in today's world, we have choices and the opportunity to do the same. We can collaborate with others and combine our ideas and resources. We can leverage our strengths and optimize advances in the tools and resources we use daily. Creating together for a better future is so important because the world is in flux right now, as portrayed by our economy and the crime in our communities. We're in need of *collective collaboration and creation* to shape where we're going next. And because collaboration is a dominant trait in most women, if we tap into our feminine power consciously, regularly, and with courage and persistence, we will be able to accelerate positive change in the world. Think about this:

- If U.S.-based, women-owned businesses were their own country, it would have the fifth largest GDP in the world, trailing closely behind Germany and ahead of countries including France, the United Kingdom, and Italy. It would also have a greater GDP

---

13  https://www.nwbc.gov/research/economic-impact-women-owned-business-es-united-states

than Canada, India, and Vietnam combined.

- There are 175 countries with fewer people than women-owned firms employ, directly and indirectly.[14]

Since women have been reclaiming and leading with their feminine power, the business world has woken up and started paying attention to what's next. Feminine power is now a recognized style, one that has its own set of skills and strategies.

When bank robbers take over banks and take hostages, people die. Or at least they used to under the old style of hostage negotiation. The old strategy of hostage negotiation involved police acting without regard to the emotional states of the robbers or their hostages. The new negotiation strategy emphasizes leading with feminine power. It places an emphasis on active listening, patience, de-escalation, empathy, and influence based on emotional factors, not force. [15]

Law enforcement, traditionally governed by the male force-forward approach to problems, is changing in many areas, primarily during hostage situations. Leading with feminine power involves listening and gathering information in an extraordinary and powerful way. Both genders have the ability to hear, but women have an extraordinary ability to listen beyond words. Many studies reference our ability to not only hear information, but to ascertain what's *not* being said. We read between the lines of what's being said through body language and other intangible means. Our abilities in this area allow us to gather and perceive information in ways that are not typically done in business or even in our day-to-day lives. Listening intently and gathering important information is an integral part of our feminine power.

Yet another aspect of our feminine power is our intuition. Research on nonverbal communication skills has clearly shown that, as a group, women are better at reading facial expressions than men. This is an

---

14 https://www.nwbc.gov/research/economic-impact-women-owned-business-es-united-states

15 https://www.psychologytoday.com/blog/beyond-words/201510/the-5-core-skills-hostage-negotiators

advantage in ways men can't even begin to imagine. Because women are more likely to pick up on subtle, emotional messages, they often make better negotiators, CEOs, human resource directors, counselors, and coaches than men.

Women don't just pick up on facial expressions. They're also better at using them to express emotions. Studies show women are better at controlling and modulating their tone of voice and body language, especially when expressing positive emotions. Men, conversely, have better poker faces, and because of a lifetime of being expected not to show emotion, they are better at hiding their feelings.

Scientific evidence shows women are more empathic than men. Women pride themselves on being more open to the emotional states of others. That openness only enhances society's impression that women have special intuitive abilities.

Of course, there are plenty of men who can read faces and emotions, too. In fact, Dr. Paul Ekman, a professor emeritus in psychology at UCSF, is a researcher and author best known for furthering our understanding of nonverbal behavior, specifically facial expressions and gestures. In 2009, Dr. Ekman was named one of the 100 most influential people in the world by *TIME* magazine, and in 2014, he ranked fifteenth amongst the most influential psychologists of the 21st century. He's best known as the man that the television show, *Lie to Me*, is based on.[16] He's a rare expert on facial expressions and acknowledges that even though men can be trained to read facial expressions, women have the edge in this field. He's not alone in recognizing that. As an article published in *Science Daily* pointed out, "[W]omen are better than men at distinguishing between emotions, especially fear and disgust, according to a new study. Scientists demonstrated that women are better than men at processing auditory, visual and audiovisual emotions."[17]

It's not just that women recognize emotions better. They also utilize their intuition more often and more accurately. Many researchers attribute this to women's primary roles throughout history as caretakers

16  http://www.paulekman.com/paul-ekman/
17  https://www.sciencedaily.com/releases/2009/10/091021125133.htm

and nurturers. Women, they say, have been "hardwired to quickly and accurately decode or detect distress in preverbal infants or threatening signals from other adults to enhance their chances at survival."[18]

Being intuitive is generally considered to be more of a female attribute than a male attribute. Women's greater sense of intuition is something that has been acknowledged for ages. It's considered a powerful attribute.

### SARAH'S STORY

When Sarah, 42, woke up at 3:00 in the morning, she immediately knew something was wrong with her 19-year-old son who was on patrol in a village during the Vietnam War.

"I don't know," she said. "It was like I heard his voice, heard him say, 'Mommy,' and then I woke up. I just knew he'd been injured." Sarah got up, dressed, made breakfast and coffee, and waited for the military to show up at her door. They appeared later that day.

"All I wanted to know was when I could see him," she said. "I knew he was alive, but in critical condition. They told me he'd been flown to Germany and that I could fly there to see him."

Intuition? Or something supernatural?

Years ago, a fire-fighting captain on a three-alarm blaze entered a room and began to wave his men into the room to fight the fire. Suddenly, he hesitated. He was surrounded by smoke and flames, which was not unusual for his job, but he could feel something was very wrong.

He waved his men out of the room and building. It collapsed into rubble and flames only seconds after the last man ran out. What did he see that saved the lives of over a dozen men? During the post fire debriefing, he said he didn't see anything unusual and it was "just firefighter's intuition." He had no conscious explanation for his decision. It wasn't until later, while under hypnosis for the PTSD he suffered from the event, that he learned what had happened.

While under hypnosis, he revealed that he'd been called to fight fires

---

18  https://www.sciencedaily.com/releases/2009/10/091021125133.htm

in the past where certain indicators, smoke and fire patterns, air pressure, sounds, and all the details that accompany or predict a collapse were noted by his brain. So, during this particular fire, his brain identified those indicators right away. As he described under hypnosis what he saw, it became very clear to him why he had made the decision he did. He clearly saw the smoke and fire patterns and felt the swell of the floor and the increase in air pressure that precedes a collapse. His subconscious knew what was happening, but his conscious mind did not.

When confronted with those signs, on a subconscious level, an "intuitive event," the urgent knowledge he needed to get out of the situation, was triggered. He didn't have time to carefully think through why he felt that way. He just *knew* they had to leave immediately or die. Call it intuition, a hunch, a gut feeling, or the subconscious at work, but the phenomenon is real.

This is similar to a woman who has been sexually assaulted in the past. When she encounters any of those same triggering events, people, smells, or locations, she may feel a strong need to leave the scene. Her brain is protecting her. Even though she has no idea why a simple smell has triggered her fear or intuition, her subconscious brain does.

Our brain begins recording events, sounds, smells, and feelings while we're still in our mother's womb. It doesn't stop until we die. Every moment, smell, sound, and event becomes part of the vast databank that helps us stay alive.

Our experiences form a record that our brain extracts information from to protect us throughout our lives. Experience is how we know hot stoves can burn us and that bee stings hurt, but it's the subconscious awareness we gain from those experiences that our brains funnel into our intuition. Intuition is a combination of instinct and reason. It's a process that gives us the ability to know something directly without conscious analytic reasoning. Intuition bridges the gap between the conscious and unconscious parts of our mind, and between instinct and reason.

Studies now show that only 20% of the brain's gray matter is dedicated to conscious thoughts, while 80% is dedicated to unconscious thoughts. Thus, tapping into that 80% of awareness would make a huge difference in our decision-making process.

We may have heard stories, for example, of mothers knowing

something was wrong with their children, as in the example given above. While we all have intuition, women have honed it in an extraordinary way. The question is not if we have it but rather how we begin to use it on a more regular basis, not just occasionally when it comes to our children.

If you're using it for your children—often one of the most important parts of a woman's life—then you certainly should feel confident using it day-to-day in your personal life and in business.

I struggle to put the last feminine power into words. It is an unmistakable power to influence that is not tangible and comes with our inner spirit. You can find it referenced in books like *The Great Cosmic Mother* or recent research from *The Future is Female.*

## BUSINESS STORY

I was speaking to a woman who is an executive at a large global organization. She talked to me about how she had presented with a colleague in front of the Board of Directors. She told me that she wore a typical grey pantsuit, created a thorough presentation with her colleague, studied her part of the material, and believed that she presented well. The person who shared this story with me was white. Her colleague was an African American woman.

Her colleague came into the same presentation with what she described as three-to-four-inch heels. She had on a colorful dress and exuded a lot of energy. She moved and occupied space as a man might, but not in the usual conservative, muted way that the board was accustomed to when operating in their corporate environment. She gave an outstanding presentation.

The Board of Directors appeared extremely engaged. They asked a lot of questions as she spoke. They followed her lead, opening up as she had, showing their concerns over a particular problem with which they were wrestling. They were able to work through that problem right then and there. The board later said that they were incredibly grateful for the information she had presented and the way in which she had presented it.

When the presentation was over, the board's boss happened to be in the room. When he gave them feedback, however, he focused exclusively on the African American woman's appearance rather than on her ability to address the board's issues. He felt that she was distracting because of the height of her heels and the colors in her dress. He made no mention of her thorough research and engaging performance.

Afterwards, my friend was talking to her colleague about the feedback, and she said "I am going to ignore that feedback because I know that I did an outstanding job. I brought my full self to this presentation, and that's why they resonated with me." Those board members were the real decision-makers, and she had no doubt that the presentation was going to have a positive impact on her career.

She succeeded, not because of her colorful dress and heels. That was a part of it, but what she was really doing was being fully herself. Her outfit was part of how she expressed herself. The energy which she used to deliver the data was a part of her full self, not a muted self she could have chosen to bring to the meeting. She decided to go with her authentic self. She had built enough confidence in the power of leading with her feminine side that she was not only successful, but also wasn't affected by the poor feedback about her outfit.

### HILLARY CLINTON

When Hillary Clinton was the Democratic nominee for President of the United States, I engaged in many conversations with some of my male colleagues about Hillary Clinton versus Donald Trump. I found it interesting that so many of the conversations revolved around her outfits and why she wore pants and not a skirt. She once wore a cape. The men and women around her thought it was voluminous and made her look too big.

I thought, "Why are we talking about this at all?" It's fascinating that the conversation went back to clothes. Hillary apparently feels more comfortable wearing pants. It's her choice of self-expression. We don't talk about Donald Trump's outfits, but we do talk about Hillary Clinton's outfits, as if it has anything to do with her qualifications.

The only correlation that should matter is how she is matching her actions as a Presidential candidate, mother, wife, and woman to her presidential platform. If your clothes and hair are in alignment with who you are, that's fantastic. Your personal preferences as to how you dress may be an interesting conversation, but really has no correlation to *how* you will lead the country.

## A SHIFT TO A FOCUS ON BEING SMART

Today, there is much more of a focus on women being smart than there ever has been. Think of Marissa Mayer, the CEO of Yahoo. She's one of the smartest women in power today, and she's not afraid to show it. Think also of the growing numbers of women attending undergraduate institutions. There's a shift in college enrollments out of high school, with Hispanic and African American women leading the charge.[19] But we also receive mixed messages on this front in both educational and business settings.

In middle school, we got messages that we should hide how smart we were. We were told to hide our brains because the boys in the class would not see us as *desirable*. Intelligence, we were told "wasn't sexy or becoming" in women. If you're in a work environment, you may have learned that when you're smart, you must not only deliberately dumb yourself down, but also do it subtly, in a way that helps everyone feel you are not in any way *grandstanding*.

So we're damned if we do and damned if we don't. But the times, they are a-changin'! Now is a time when, as women, we're giving ourselves permission to be smart and unapologetic about it.

What's really great about this attribute is it's not just about our intelligence. Being smart totally rocks, but when we combine our smarts with our intuition, our feminine power packs an even greater punch.

I see women in the media who are taking a lead, such as Katty Kay and Claire Shipman on BBC and ABC news, respectively. Now is the time when we're giving ourselves permission to be smart, use those attributes, and not cover them up.

*"Many women will find it hard to believe, but new research suggests that*

---

19 http://www.pewresearch.org/fact-tank/2014/03/06/

*men increasingly value intellect and character in a partner over a shapely figure."* [20]

You're definitely still going to see an emphasis on beautiful women. Men are hardwired to be visual creatures and respond to beauty. However, more and more, the age of the smart, competent, and courageous woman is asserting itself. This shift from beauty to brains will help women, particularly young women, as they are promoted more quickly because of their skills. Maybe that period when young girls change between childhood and teen years will cease to exist, leaving a roadway for them to just keep soaring with their authentic selves, all different and reveling in those differences.

Giving the opportunity to girls to be all that they can be is exciting. It's time for us to get involved in this important cause.

## BENEFITS OF DIVERSE WORKPLACES

In 2016, 60% of university graduates in Europe and North America were women. According to a book called *Why Women Mean Business*, companies with women in more leadership positions are outperforming those with fewer.

Studies also show that companies that adapt to women and female qualities in their culture have a better workforce, greater productivity, and better problem-solving capabilities. While there's little correlation between a group's collective intelligence and the IQs of its individual members, if a group includes more women, its collective intelligence rises. According to researchers, the most valuable skill is not group or individual intelligence, but social sensitivity, something women have in far greater amounts than men do. [21]

This translates into the reality that diverse workplaces are much more capable of attracting our younger generations. They're also better able to

---

20  http://www.pewresearch.org/fact-tank/2014/03/06/womens-college-enrollment-gains-leave-men-behind/

21  https://hbr.org/2011/06/defend-your-research-what-makes-a-team-smarter-more-women/

integrate those who are close to retirement. Additionally, they're able to leverage diversity in significant ways that hit their bottom line. For example, "A diverse workforce can capture a greater share of the consumer market."[22]

## MATURITY

Studies show that girls mature faster than boys on many levels. Their brains develop sooner, and their social skills and emotional intelligence is often years or even decades ahead of their male counterparts. Smarts matter, but social skills, social sensitivity, emotional intelligence, and maturity often make the biggest difference.

Men succeed with less intelligence, maturity, and social sensitivity because they've been taught from an early age to have confidence, act in spite of fear, and believe in themselves. Studies back this up. Men succeed in spite of their incompetence because confidence is as critical a factor in success as competence.[23]

According to a May 2014 article in *The Atlantic*:

*In the United States, women now earn more college and graduate degrees than men do. We make up half the workforce, and we are closing the gap in middle management. Half a dozen global studies, conducted by the likes of Goldman Sachs and Columbia University, have found that companies employing women in large numbers outperform their competitors on every measure of profitability. Our competence has never been more obvious. Those who closely follow society's shifting values see the world moving in a female direction.[24]*

So why are men still getting hired, promoted faster, and making more

---

22  https://www.americanprogress.org/issues/economy/news/2012/07/12/11900/the-top-10-economic-facts-of-diversity-in-the-workplace/

23  https://www.theatlantic.com/magazine/archive/2014/05/the-confidence-gap/359815/

24  https://www.theatlantic.com/magazine/archive/2014/05/the-confidence-gap/359815/

money than women? Because women still lack confidence. For instance, Katty Kay got a degree from a top university. She speaks several languages and is one of the most recognized women in America. Yet she attributes her media success more to the fact she has an English accent and less to the fact she's a brilliant journalist. She admits in various interviews that she spent much of her life convinced that she just wasn't intelligent enough to compete for the most prestigious jobs in journalism.

Before her book *Lean In* was published, the COO of Facebook, Sheryl Sandberg, told interviewers, "There are still days I wake up feeling like a fraud, not sure I should be where I am."

The crisis for women isn't skills, maturity, or feminine power. The thing holding us back is a confidence gap. *The Atlantic* continues:

> *Compared with men, women don't consider themselves as ready for promotions, they predict they'll do worse on tests, and they generally underestimate their abilities. This disparity stems from factors ranging from upbringing to biology. A growing body of evidence shows just how devastating this lack of confidence can be.*[25]

The good news is that confidence can be taught and learned. We can close the gap. Other women have done it, and you can too.

### PROCESS

The process starts where we started at the beginning of this book. It's all about knowing yourself and your values. Research shows that when you are aware of your own values, you are far more successful in life than you would be if you're not connected to your values. Even if you're in an environment where someone else's values are different from your own, if you are clear about what your values are, you need not prove anything or debate with people about who is right or wrong.

You also will have less confusion around why someone without your

---

25  https://www.theatlantic.com/magazine/archive/2014/05/the-confi-dence-gap/359815/

values did what he or she did. Instead, you stay solidly planted in your values. You're able to clearly see what is going on around you. Add confidence to that and the ability to stand firmly behind your values, and you have the foundations for untold success.

So, as I pointed out, **Step One** is just knowing who you are. Below is an exercise from Melissa's process of networking that starts with figuring out your top four values.

**Step Two** is to recognize the impact of qualities you have that perhaps, in the past, have not always been seen in a positive light, such as intuition or strong listening skills. Understand the value of intuition. Understand the value of hearing and gathering information that others may not see. Understand the value of having not only intuition, but also a vision for the future – not just for your company and your family, but one for the world. Then take responsibility to help that vision come to fruition.

**Step Three** is to understand that you are part of the current state of the world and that you have the strength to address some or many of its problems. As we go through this paradigm shift from a patriarchal to more of a feminine environment, change is not always the most comfortable thing. But you are here at this time for a reason. This is a part of your role. Sometimes you won't like what's happening. You will feel alone because you'll be leading a change initiative that the people around you might not see the need for. Know that you are okay. That's how every leader feels.

When you're giving birth, no one can give birth but you. No matter how much someone else loves you, they can't give birth to your baby. The personal shift that's taking place, which is part of a collective shift, is yours alone to create. The end result is worth your temporary pain. The outcome on the other side—for society, your family, and your organization—will be far greater than the temporary pain you might feel.

# CHAPTER EIGHT

# Secret #6: Shift Into Extreme Self-Care

Extreme self-care entails taking the time to go into a serene and beautiful environment where you let go and become your best self. It may seem counterintuitive that by *letting go* you put yourself in the best place to receive.

Self-care is about creating time just for you. Some people find that having an *accountability partner* or an *inspiration partner* can be helpful. It might also mean hiring a coach to make sure you keep your commitment to yourself.

You could also consider joining a mastermind group, which is a group of about ten to fifteen people who spend time together supporting one another through ongoing face-to-face or online sessions to meet their respective goals. In today's world, too many of our connections are through the internet. We need more one-to-one or small group connections where we have the opportunity to share more of our aspirations and challenges.

As Gladwell pointed out in *The Tipping Point*, you can't have any more than fifteen truly connected relationships in your life at any one time. Any more than fifteen and your mental/physical connection bandwidth would be on overdrive. When you spend time on sites like Facebook, for example, you may find yourself, as so many do today, experiencing bouts of depression that stem from loneliness. You may wonder why you feel so alone when you have access to lots of people. It's because they, too, are reaching out, and the result is a lot of noise rather than the regular, steady attention you could get from more intimate conversations. Unfortunately, the loneliness epidemic that's occurring only seems to be spreading. There are studies that show that people get depressed as a result of being on social media because they often only put up their best moments, so it seems like everyone has amazing lives and they don't. Realize that what you are viewing is only a very small piece of someone's life.

The answers aren't easy, but this secret to effective self-care entails figuring out two things: 1) what you can do by yourself, and 2) what you can do with one other person or a small group to feed your spirit, your heart, and your mind.

## KEYS TO UNLOCK THIS POWER

Start by creating something like an inspiration journal where you can write daily about what inspired you that day. Carry this with you throughout your day. Use it to help you notice when you're feeling the happiest. For example, you may find that sitting on a park bench just watching people play with their kids or pets brings you a sense of peace and calm. Write that insight down. Or you might find that taking a walk around your neighborhood or nearby lake is where you start to get ideas for overcoming some of the roadblocks you are finding in your daily work.

Many times, we're not cognizant unless we make a point of creating a process for ourselves to discover what it is that *makes us tick*. It's hard to project backwards as to what *made* us happy. It's far easier to take the time to explore using tools like a journal or your phone to document those inspired moments. Then you can begin to lead your life rather than having your life lead you.

We have such a hard time being aware of what makes us happy or unhappy. Take the journal around for a week, and mark the times when you find yourself in a moment close to bliss. Mark those moments and then keep referencing them. You may find that you transition from being unconscious to the things that bring you joy to being in tune with them and, ultimately, with your own happiness. It's your *What Makes*

*Me Tick* moments. Once you know what you want, you can start moving toward your destiny to achieve those dreams.

Then, you can get another notebook. Try an unlined one where you can draw pictures. Don't forget to draw yourself in each picture. Then *imagine*. Here, see yourself in the picture. Get curious. For example, one client of mine had the following epiphany:

> *I was there on a park bench in a nearby park I like to visit. I found myself so relaxed as I saw a group of two beautiful golden retrievers, one an older dog, the other a puppy. I kept watching the two of them playing, and I felt a sense of joy and peace I haven't felt in such a long time. I realized that maybe someday I'll have a dog. Maybe, for now, I'll go volunteer at the local shelter and play with the dogs.*

You start to then see what's possible, and you try it. It's the dip-your-toe-in-the-water moment before you decide to just jump right in. Acclimate yourself to experience joy when you're by yourself. What are those joyful moments? What's your perfect day like?

Write it out in your journal. You may have to do this several days in a row or talk it through with someone else. It can take a while to figure this out because we can get so wrapped up in our routines that we need to step back and look at ourselves from an outsider's perspective in order to realize what matters to us. But, once you figure out *all the many things* that light you up, you will be able to make those things happen more regularly. It's about taking the time to discover the things that will get easier to figure out when you take up journaling.

When you find yourself feeling low, you can go back to your journal and read your inspiration entries to lift yourself up. That's the one-on-one piece. You must live in the moment and recognize all the possibilities that exist for you in the future.

I think about the two weeks that I just had. They were highly stressful and busy, filled with travel and all the frustration and exhaustion that comes with it. I was not practicing extreme self-care. I wonder if I were more in the habit of self-care, would I have done some things differently even in the midst of my busy weeks? Fifteen minutes of sun. If I had taken just fifteen minutes to be in the sun, could I have gotten energy from that experience? It also would have been helpful to have some sort of self-soothing system. For me, it might just be rubbing the dog. By my house, there is an Asian massage establishment. It's really unique. They do the massages in recliner chairs, and you can get it done quickly or you can do a regular full body massage. That could be a regular self-soothing thing for me because it could be as short as fifteen minutes.

## GIVE YOUR FEELINGS A RATING

Even ten minutes of mindful attention to your feelings can help. Don't wait until the end of your day to realize "Oh, my God. It's been horrible."

Try giving your feelings a rating from 1-5, from best to worst. For example:

1. I'm awesome! This is going to be a great day!

2. I'm feeling rather good. I'm not ecstatic, but I have a sense of hope and am looking forward to what the day brings.

3. I'm okay. I'll muddle through the day. I just wish I felt happier.

4. I'm depressed or stressed, but I'm mobile. I'll muscle through the day, but I *wish* I didn't have to show my face in public.

5. I'm feeling so depressed or very stressed. I feel like I want to just go bury my head in my pillow and not come out of bed for days.

Keep checking on your feelings using the above scale every hour or two so that if you find yourself at a 3 or under, you make an effort to move yourself back up the scale.

## ONE-TO-ONE

One of the things that prevents women from extreme self-care is the quiet commitments that we have with some of our family, friends, and colleagues. These can divert our attention from self-care. Some commitments might be picking up your friend's kids or their dry-cleaning. You may have to go out of your way to do these things, but, well, they *are* your friends. But sometimes, these commitments get out of hand. "Yes, friend, I will go to lunch with you today because you need to talk." We all want to be good friends and family members.

But there are things we commit to that we don't want to, and, suddenly, we are sabotaging our commitment to our extreme self-care. As an example, I have a good friend that I do some business with as well. She is consistently late and neglectful of doing her part. If we're working on a project and I'm going to do A through C and she's going to do D through F, I'll come with A through C and she'll do D, but not E and not F. Then she'll say, "Let's just go ahead and co-create E and F."

Of course, because we're co-creating, it turns out fine. But the quiet commitment is that because we're friends, I'm supposed to pick up her slack, and because we're partners, have an understanding of co-creation.

Extreme self-care in your relationships is about recognizing where you have these quiet commitments with people. Then you have to re-evaluate those commitments and ultimately decide which commitments to end and which to keep. In my case, it might not be worth keeping up my quiet commitment to do my friend's unfinished work because it consistently takes time away from my practice of extreme self-care.

## WORK FATIGUE SYNDROME—BURNOUT

I was working with a client at a municipality right outside of Chicago. We were talking about doing leadership and supervisory training, and we observed how some of the leaders know what to do in terms of developing their direct reports and giving feedback, holding people accountable, and helping with engagement. But they just weren't doing it.

I asked my client contact Stefan Johnson – one of the more senior leaders there – what he thought was going on. He said it was supervisory fatigue. When I asked him, he explained that, since this was a police department of a municipality, they were just tired. They're working every day in a physical job. To add to that, when it came to the other jobs that they should be doing – people and business and process-related things – they were just tired from doing these things year after year and not necessarily seeing the result. After a while, they feel like, "Forget it. I'm just going to do the bare minimum."

I tried to take that concept and expand it to a corporate environment – to my own experiences and the experiences of others – and I observed that many times, when you're at a middle management level or in that first real leadership position, you get tired. Not only are we being asked to do more with less money and fewer resources, but also to deal effectively with our daily office politics. There's a level of emotional drain that comes from working hard and not getting the appreciation that you feel you deserve. Or that emotional drain may come from the consistent stress and strain of trying to do your job well every day and being mindful of the lives in your hands.

If you are a parent or guardian, and play a significant role in an organization outside of your home, it's a lot to balance. If you've made it to a middle manager level or above, it's likely that you've been running at a fast pace with a lot of stress for 15 to 30 years. After a while, if you haven't figured out a way to consistently rejuvenate yourself and maintain some level of balance, you get tired. Most of us wait until we're absolutely exhausted, and then take that vacation once or twice a year. There's this cumulative effect of fatigue, and we start to wonder, "Why am I this way? Last week" (or last month, or last year) "wasn't that bad." We don't consider that we've been running the last fifteen years at that particular pace.

Fatigue plays a role in how well you can accomplish extreme self-care. Note that fatigue is not just something that happens to you today, or this week, but is actually an *accumulation* of days, weeks, and even months when you experience fatigue. At some point, you end up hitting a *tipping point* of fatigue.

How do you combat this? One way is to do a midyear checkup regarding supervisory fatigue. I might even say a quarterly checkup. Midyear can be too late.

Following is an assessment I created to help determine your current level of fatigue:

**ASSESSMENT FOR WORK FATIGUE SYNDROME**

1.  I don't feel supported because others don't relate to me.

2.  I find myself with so many demands on my time that I have trouble finding the time to connect.

3.  I have difficulty pinpointing the variety of things that bother me.

4.  I find myself getting anxious and don't know why this feeling came on.

5.  I feel there is always another bar for me to reach and I don't take the time to just be satisfied with where I am ... RIGHT NOW.

6.  I have a sense of urgency to *Do, Do, Do* rather than just BE.

7.  I don't know the step or steps I can take to change my current trajectory.

8.  I want so much more than what I'm receiving right now.

9.  I find myself fighting loneliness regularly even though there are plenty of people around.

10. I have BIG DREAMS but, right now, my passion to achieve them is growing smaller because I'm putting my energy into things that don't hold high, positive energy. I'm losing my passion.

If you answered yes to more than four of the above questions, you are experiencing fatigue. However, levels of fatigue can vary, so it's important to know where you're at.

**LEVELS OF FATIGUE**

*Level 1*

You start to feel physically tired. Maybe you are not sleeping as well because your brain is constantly in distress and that tends to keep you up. You start to hear from your friends – social friends or friends at work – that they haven't seen you lately. "Hey, I missed you at *this*." "We didn't see you at lunch." "You didn't come to the reception." That sort of thing. You might be seeing some occasional mistakes, but nothing major. You feel it physically, and your pep talks to yourself are something like, "I just need to push through. I just need to get through this project. I'm going to catch up on my sleep this weekend." It doesn't look like anything major, but there are physical signs, comments from others who notice, and, at least subconsciously, you yourself have realized it.

*Level 2*

You've experienced everything from Level 1, but now you are consciously focused on the fact that you are tired. You recognize that something's going on. You feel physically tired. Emotionally, you're a little short with people, not as patient. Maybe you're starting to feel overly sensitive. You are actively thinking things like, "I'm going to take that vacation in three months." You make plans in your head, but they aren't *now* plans. They're future plans. "I'm going to take that vacation. I am going to pass this work off to this direct report. I am going to have this meeting with my boss about *X, Y* and *Z*."

Your social circle now knows that you're not going to make certain events, but you tell them that it's temporary until you get through tax season, or this project, or until the new president has been named at the company.

You are acutely aware because you feel it physically and emotionally. You tell yourself, "We've been through this before. We're really strong. We can work through this. This is a part of leadership. This is a part of being a mother." Your plan for relief is future-based.

# Secret #6: Shift Into Extreme Self-Care

## *Level 3*

That mindset in Level 2 becomes a way a life. Of course, you're going to take a vacation at some point, but it's no longer top of mind. You might have just become numb to some things happening around you because there's so much going on that you don't have the energy for all of it. You are on automatic. It has become normal that you are not sleeping as much because of work or what's going on subconsciously in your brain. You are likely out of the loop with your social events and, if you go, you most often go just out of obligation. Even if you're going for a good time, it's hard for you to cut it off.

You are starting to have physical ailments. They probably started in Level 2, but now you have physical ailments to the point that you are going to the doctor about it. Maybe it's chest pains, severe back pains, consistent headaches, or circulation problems. Maybe they can't find anything. "You've been here a couple of times, but we aren't seeing anything. What's going on with your stress or anxiety?"

Or, they do see it. Some level is elevated, and you commit to working on it. But you don't really do it because you don't have time.

In this Level 3, you might also find yourself having a heart attack or stroke. You might have an extreme anxiety attack. You may sleep for some inordinate amount of time when you actually take time off.

Level 3 is starting to impact your life. You're still effective by all accounts, still a high performer, but perhaps the way that you used to develop people is not as apparent unless they have high potential. You aren't as nurturing with family and friends as you were before, and your general level of enthusiasm has shifted because you're in a crisis at work on a consistent basis.

### THINGS TO DO TO START ADDRESSING FATIGUE

If you answered yes to more than four of the above questions, you are experiencing fatigue. At this point, it's time to take steps to address your fatigue with as much self-care as possible. Here are some suggestions:

- **Eat healthy, *small* snacks throughout the day.** Studies show that eating small quantities of nutritious snacks every couple of hours helps keep your metabolism moving and prevents sugar spikes.

- **Get plenty of sleep.** Study after study shows that one of the best things we can do for our health is to get a good amount of sleep each night. According to the Mayo Clinic, the suggested number of hours you need for a good night's rest is seven. [26]

- **Find someone to talk to regularly.** Find a supportive colleague or friend with whom you can regularly *defrag* as I term it. It's often better, in fact, if this person is not part of your regular personal life network. This way you both can feel comfortable sharing things that won't seep into your homelife.

### ADDRESSING SUPERVISORY FATIGUE

- Make sure to take the assessments

- 30 days make a habit around self-care

- Rewards/acknowledgements

The other thing is to reconnect with your *Why*. When I was going through fatigue, I discovered that I was doing a lot of stuff that I really didn't love or even like. All the stuff that I felt like maybe I didn't love but were a means to an end had gone out of my head. I was functioning on automatic. It was helpful for me to reconnect with my *Why* because that allowed me to prioritize differently, tolerate some of the stuff that I felt like I had to do for just a little bit longer because it got me to my *Why*. It made it easier for me to drop some other things that didn't fit with my *Why*.

Reconnecting with my *Why* rejuvenated my motivation, bringing

26  http://www.mayoclinic.org/healthy-lifestyle/adult-health/in-depth/sleep/art-20048379

energy back to where I was spending my time and why. It got me excited about what I was doing again.

# CHAPTER NINE

# Secret #7: Imagination

Imagination is more important than knowledge. Knowledge is limited, whereas imagination is infinite, it stimulates progress and gives birth to evolution.

In knowledge management, one of the big ah-ha moments is that you don't know what you don't know. The same is true for imagination. Imagination releases you to embrace the entirety of existence and beyond. Stimulating its progress is innovation. Innovation is beyond the fuel. It's the superfuel that makes companies and people great, giving them the power to tap into their imaginative potential. It doesn't just make people and their companies run. It causes both to excel far beyond their wildest dreams. It makes everything exponentially better.

Everyone is free to create his world as he wants it if he knows that the whole thing is responding to him.[27] This simply means that there is nothing that's happening to you that you didn't first perceive as possible. What you see is based on the intensity of your imagination. I'll share a brief story. Some years ago I owned a mortgage company with two other gentlemen. We were wildly successful initially and after about two years lost everything. The details are not important but I found myself living in DC away from my family, struggling to eat, and living in temporary housing. On this particular day, I was living in a big empty home that my friend's friend owned. The house was on the market and my friend

---

27 Neville Goddard, *The Law And Other Essays on Manifestations*. Wilder Publications (February 25, 2011)

talked his friend in allowing me to stay there for $200 a month until it sold. I had absolutely no food. I felt I had tapped on my friend's kindness enough so I didn't want to ask them for any help. At this point I had become accustomed to eating once a day but on this day I didn't even have that. However, I decided to put to use what I know at this point I really had no choice. I showered, got dressed, put on make-up and sat on the bed. I envisioned eating steak, my favorite, I felt what it was like to be full, I smiled about it and then I literally sat on the bed and waited. I didn't have a steady job so I had no where else to go. Within about 20 minutes a friend of mine called who did not have a car. I luckily still had a working BMW. He said if I would pick him up and take him to the grocery store and cook him dinner that he would buy me groceries. Of course this was a no-brainer. I picked him up, he bought me groceries that lasted about a month, and I made him what else, "steak" and a baked potato for dinner at his request. I have had this experience through using my imagination more times than I can tell you. Now you might be thinking "well how come you aren't a millionaire" or "why don't you have everything you desire out of life" well the answer is I'm on my way. The other point is that it only works when you can imagine what you desire to the exclusion of anything else. So often there is problem that causes us to desire what we desire. In our imagining what we tend to focus on is the problem not what you have imagined. Or we consistently tell ourselves that what we want isn't possible and we get into the mode of trying to figure out "how" it's going to happen versus having faith in the power of imagination itself. I have used my imagination to experience amazing relationships and ruin others. I've used it to get great business contracts and make others business relationships very challenging. Imagination is impersonal and responds to your ongoing dominant thoughts and feelings.

If this is true, it behooves us to be in a place to create imagination sessions. We must, therefore, ask questions that push us to innovative solutions.

My colleague, Melissa G. Wilson, wrote an incredibly useful book called *75 Cage Rattling Questions to Change the Way You Work* in which she explained a process that uses the acronym ASK, as follows:

# Secret #7: Imagination

## A: AWAKEN WITH A QUESTION

Come up with a question to begin the process of stimulating your imagination. Examples of questions could be:

- What's a question I'm not asking currently?

- Who can I turn to who isn't in my field for a different perspective on my current problem?

- What's one thing I can do today that would help me accomplish something I've been putting off doing?

## S: SPIN OUT WITH MORE AND BETTER QUESTIONS

Melissa was called in to work with a team of people at a major advertising firm. They were consultants who never had to sell their services before, but now their organization was asking them to bring in business. Suddenly, they were responsible for finding new business and closing deals – a very different role for them than their creative work required. Of course, they had a hard time because they were in a place that is often termed "conscious incompetence." They weren't great salespeople ... yet.

Melissa went into her "Questioneering Session" as she termed it, and the first question put to her was "What can we do to make it easier for us to sell? We're consultant-creatives, and all of a sudden we have to sell. What do we do?"

Beginning with the imagination stage of "Awaken with a Question," the consultants were able to spark a variety of possibilities for new consulting. Moving on to the stage of "Spin Out with More and Better Questions," they continued to develop questions such as "What if we were able to double our current revenues with new business? How might we make that happen?"

This second round of questions got everyone excited about the potential of new, interesting business. They were then able to move to the third part of the process, the stage of "Kindle and Ignite with Action Questions." Here, the team moved to their left-brain analytical sides and worked out a variety of next steps they could each take to move through their network of people and explore getting introductions to new business opportunities.

Another idea that emerged in the "K" stage was for the group to work together on sales calls. There are studies that show how putting junior salespeople into small teams can help them learn to better manage the pressures of the sales environment and succeed faster because of this approach.

Going through the ASK process puts lots of opportunities into play. Once the actions happen, they produce questions like "When are we going to come back again to inspire each other and share our success stories?"

Knowledge is limited. There is a saying that goes "You don't know what you don't know." But going beyond your current knowledge and pushing through with questions moves you to a space of imagination. Throughout this book, I've been inviting you to harness your imagination and put it into a process to get the most out of your own unique creative power. I believe a process like the one above will help you and those around you get unstuck and fully explore new worlds of possibility.

We can all learn from each other's successes. You gain leverage from your strengths, not your weaknesses. You have a power within you that you've been given to use. It's your imagination. It's like talking directly to God, or whatever higher being you believe in, who says, "If you can see it in your imagination, you can actually make it happen."

We can use a classic thought experiment from quantum physics to demonstrate this point. The double slit experiment, originally performed by American physicists Clinton Davisson and Lester Germer in 1927, demonstrated how a light source, such as a beam of light, can pass through a plate pierced by two parallel slits. This then will produce a light on a screen behind the plate. Davisson and Lester predicted that they would see a light pattern on the screen corresponding to the size and shape of the slits on the plate. But instead, the light produced a diffraction pattern of light and dark bands. This was an unexplained phenomenon at the time, as light was thought to travel in waves. What Davisson and Lester *expected* to see was much different from what they *actually* saw. In fact, they believed what they witnessed to be impossible!

## Secret #7: Imagination

So it is with the power of imagination. Often, we limit ourselves to what we think is possible and work within that safe, secure space. But we aren't truly tapping into the potential of our imagination. If you do use the ASK process, explained above (especially the Spin step), you will open yourself to new ideas and begin down a vibrant path to manifesting more in your life. And once you open the flood gates of focused imagination through the power of great questions, you will find yourself in a wonderful new space of possibility. You will also find what you need to reach your goals.

***

In *The Tipping Point*, Malcolm Gladwell's critically-acclaimed book exploring "that magic moment when an idea, trend, or social behavior crosses a threshold, tips, and spreads like wildfire," he discusses three different archetypes of change makers: mavens, sales people, and connectors. Mavens make change happen through ideas and knowledge. Sales people make change happen through persuasion. And connectors make change happen through people. Gladwell discusses these as three separate models, implying that we can only be one of these if we seek to make change.

But I believe we can be a combination of two or even three of these archetypes. Omitting this possibility is symptomatic of the rudimentary level of networking that still exists in most business environments. We can learn to better recognize these archetypes in ourselves and others and leverage them with some help. Some organizations have discovered that they need to evolve from bringing in consultants and trainers to bringing in coaches and facilitators. That's a higher level of discernment in an organization, one that is much more hands on, much more directed, and much more focused on people who want to make change happen on multiple fronts.

To create that internal ecosystem, that "intrapreneurial" or imagination-centered environment, you need a facilitator who gets this. Once the imagination is developed and turned into a process for the organization to innovate, then it's turned into your knowledge, and ultimately, a higher form of knowledge is wisdom. Here, you can leverage your mavens and their knowledge to create change, while also linking them to their sales and connector sides and those who identify with those archetypes.

## WHAT YOU CAN YOU DO TOMORROW TO BRING IMAGINATION INTO YOUR PERSONAL LIFE AND YOUR BUSINESS LIFE

- Don't take yourself so seriously! Remember that each day is a gift, and gifts bring beauty, knowledge, and love into our lives.

- Search for beautiful quotes on the internet and print them out so you have a mantra each day, and live out the day around that inspiring quote.

- A lot of people don't know that on sites like *Goodreads*, you can search under "imagination" and find over 200 quotes from books on this topic. Once you go deep, instead of running out of or low on inspiration, it will grow exponentially! You open up all sorts of possibilities and create a "shoot for the stars" mentality. When you're there, you're open to creation. When you're open to creation, possibilities appear and serendipities occur.

- Find images that inspire you. So many of us are visual learners, stimulated by photos and drawings rather than printed words. Get video clips of the most beautiful places on earth. The mind will connect to that. Use these as a five-minute break in your day. Have them prepared in advance for those moments when you can take a break, you're feeling down, or you have some anxiety. This will reset your brain and ease stress. Some people even put a rubber band around their wrist or set a timer on their watch to remind them to take time for themselves – and their imagination – throughout the day.

- Write one page of positive notes to yourself each day. Some of you can do this easily on your morning commute; others may find it helpful to do it first thing in the morning. Take a few moments, and jot down a few bullet points, focusing on anything good that has happened to you recently or the positive, imaginative work you wish to accomplish that day. Mantras are also a great way to establish positive motivation. Then, go back to this page throughout the day and reinforce the positive notes. Say, "I did a good job with this." The next one could be, "Talk to yourself nicely," or "Don't be so hard on yourself."

- Three times a day, take a few minutes to have what I call "imagination sessions."

  - In the morning before you get out of bed, before you really get started and thinking about all the stuff you've got to do, use those few minutes between being asleep and fully awake to imagine the most positive day possible. Think about this most ideal day without any filters. Feel what that would be like. Even if you have no idea how that would possibly, show up, do it anyway because it's a freeing experience. What will happen is you'll get a lot closer to that ideal than you would if you only focused on the average or expected.
  - Then, in the middle of the day, reconnect with that thinking and imagine how you want the rest of your day to go. Leave behind how the day has gone so far – focus on positivity and imaginative possibility for what's ahead.
  - Finally, right before you go to bed, imagine what a fantastic night's sleep feels like and how you will enter tomorrow full of positivity and wonder. Try to do this right before you fall asleep so it really gets into your subconscious. This exercise frees you from what *is*, letting the power that exists in imagination to work and release what *can and will be*.

For those who might be uncomfortable or unfamiliar with how to start these exercises, or those who cannot break free from the familiar, I would just pick one and concentrate on that exercise for a few weeks. Write yourself a note every day, including weekends; print out 2-3 visuals and hang them in places where you will see them frequently. If you're trying the "imagination sessions" and it's just not working, scale it back a bit. Start by asking yourself basic questions. Think, "What would happen if this one thing were to take place? What would it look like if this did take place? How would my life change?" Do that to start the day, and do it again in the evening before bed. Once you've established a routine and have begun to open your mind to these possibilities, you can begin incorporating more "imagination sessions" with even more positive questions throughout your day.

# CHAPTER 10

# *What's Next?*

You've learned about the power of your metaphorical vault and the precious gifts and skills you keep within you. You've discovered the seven secrets to feminine power: your superpowers, your network, creating your own reality, proper perspective, leading with feminine power, extreme self-care, and your imagination. You've begun to understand the value in each secret, and how, when taken together, they can help you realize your fullest potential.

Now, I'd like to provide you with my top ten ways to use these secrets *right now*. Yes, now! You have all the tools you need to produce greatness in your life, from the inside out. With this great power, comes great responsibility. Use it wisely and reveal your Golden Buddha to the world.

## TOP TEN WAYS TO TAKE ACTION NOW

1. **Know your worth.** You are an important member of your workplace and a precious family member and friend. Realize your talents and how much you have to offer. You are worthy of happiness and deserve all that you want to accomplish.

2. **Identify role models.** Find empowered female role models who can help guide you and provide inspiration for your goals, lifestyle, and methods of self-care. Role models can be anyone, a public figure you respect or someone close to you. Identify what you like about them or their methods of working, and try to adopt some of these methods as your own.

3. **Know your boundaries**. Stay true to yourself. Don't let other people try to convince you to do something you don't want to do. You'll just end up unhappy and off-track.

4. **Expand your boundaries**. Get to know people outside of your usual social circle. Try to interact with different types of people. They will broaden your horizons and share outlooks on life that you might have never considered. You never know what doors these relationships could open and what opportunities could be created.

5. **Evaluate your relationships and build a support system.** Recognize which relationships are positive forces in your life and which relationships are toxic. Toxic relationships will only cause you sadness and problems, and distract you from your goals. Identify these fake friends and remove them from your life. In turn, take time to be with the people who matter. Family and friends who are positive parts of your life deserve to be celebrated and cherished. Take time to strengthen these relationships. The stronger these relationships, the stronger your support system.

6. **Don't lose track of your goals.** Every day ask yourself: what can I do today to bring myself one step closer to achieving my goals? Make sure that you accomplish something, no matter how small, that works towards your goals. Consider visualizing your goals. Visualizing your goals coming to fruition will motivate you to work towards them.

7. **Embrace vulnerability**. Some things are out of your control and might not always go the way you expect them to. Embrace the process and don't have a negative mindset about vulnerability. Instead, think of it as an exciting and authentic part of life.

8. **Take breaks.** Whether you take an hour break to clear your head during a busy day or a two-week vacation to relax and

recharge, breaks are important. They are beneficial to your mental health and happiness, and allow you to tackle your work with fresh motivation. Incorporate scheduled breaks into your routine to ensure you take them.

9. **Be gentle with yourself.** If something goes wrong, don't punish yourself. Mistakes are inevitable. Stay calm, refocus, and construct a plan to fix what went wrong.

10. **Lastly ... Never. Give. Up.** There will be obstacles in the way of your goals. Maybe you won't achieve your goals as quickly as you think you should. Be patient, keep working, and believe in yourself. Your efforts will pay off.

### BEFORE YOU GO

If you found this book useful, please let me know by visiting my website at www.theerikawalker.com. I welcome all your thoughts and suggestions. Note that also on my site I will share extra resources with you.

Also, please consider putting up a review on Amazon. The review doesn't have to be long. Even three sentences will do. Reviews matter greatly as they indicate to people that a book is worth reading. They truly make or break an author. So, if you did like what you read, please share it. Amazon is the best location to put up a review because more than 80% of all books are sold there.

Finally, thank you. I appreciate you. You made a difference in my life by reading this book. I sincerely hope that it made a difference in your life, too, and that you will spread the insights you got from this book and gift it by passing on your new wisdom—even this or another copy of this book—to someone you care about.

# *Acknowledgements*

I want to acknowledge my parents who provided me unwavering support so that I could pursue the things I love. I also thank them both for putting me in a metaphysical church at an early age to learn spiritual and scientific principles that have carried me through my life. I want to acknowledge my aunts, uncles, and cousins who have been more like siblings to me as an only child. Thank you!

There are men and women who have been a tremendous amount of support and joy in each phase of my life, far too many to mention. However, there are a few that I have enjoyed triple decade friendships with who I want to acknowledge because it is blessing to have friends that long. They are truly integrated throughout the pages of my story. Those friends are: Kimberly Roberts, LaShare Edwards, Stefan Johnson, Karen Clay, LaTicia White, Cheryl Pierson, Herb Long, Eugene Sadler, Mallori Alise Lockett, Michael Luster and Jane Elizabeth. I want to also acknowledge Derrick Graham who made his transition before this book was complete but was such an inspiration and support in me expressing my personal power.

Anyone who has birthed a book for the first time will tell you that there are unexpected emotions and sometimes an eerie silence that happens throughout the process. Therefore, I would have not been able to complete this book without the love, support, and know-how of my Publishing Partner, Melissa G. Wilson.

Education is so important, yet so much of what you learn in school is not in the classroom but the access it provides, the culture you're immersed in, and the greatness of the people! I would be remiss if I did not acknowledge the two schools that shaped me the most: Kenwood Academy and Howard University. You are always in my heart.

Lastly, I must acknowledge the two true loves of my life: Chassity and Afo, my dogs. They provide unconditional love and the greatest feedback! ☺

Erika